REAL FLOW

Break the Burnout Cycle and Unlock High Performance in the New World of Work

STAR BLAZER PRESS

Contact information for Star Blazer Press– info@starblazerpress.com
www.starblazerpress.com

ISBN: 979-8-218-01842-9 (paperback)
ISBN: 979-8-218-01843-6 (ebook)

Ordering Information:
Special discounts are available on quantity purchases by corporations, associations, and others. For details, contact info@starblazerpress.com +1 651-212-4155

REAL FLOW

Break the Burnout Cycle and Unlock High
Performance in the New World of Work

Brandi Olson

WARNING

Once you read this book, you will not be able to unlearn what you have read. You will see it everywhere and in every facet of the work you are doing. You will no longer be satisfied with the level of performance that your organization has been able to achieve up to this point. You will realize that you, your organization, and the people at the center of it have been settling for expectations that are far too low and an amount of stress that is far too high. And you will find the *relief* you've been looking for.

TABLE OF CONTENTS

CHAPTER ONE

STUCK IN THE FLOOD

I WAS STANDING IN THREE feet of cold, rushing water and trying desperately not to lose the feeling in my feet. After all, they were the only thing keeping me upright. One wrong move and the river would take me away.

To my right was my paddle, while to my left was my kayak, its tip jammed between two rocks. The more the water rushed, the farther my paddle drifted away, and the more stuck my kayak became.

It was the second time that day that I had been separated from my paddle, so to say I was frustrated was an understatement.

But I had known what I was getting into when I had launched into the water that morning, and I had done it anyway.

Most of the time, the *Amnicon* River in northern Wisconsin moves at a quick but manageable speed and has a few challenging white-water rapids. It's a difficult but fun course, and when the water is right, I can usually paddle my favorite stretch in about four hours.

But in the spring, the river changes.

The snow melts up north, which causes an intense flood of water to migrate into the river. Suddenly, my usual demanding but feasible stretch of water becomes a raging monster. The river bed gets overwhelmed by the amount of water, and the entire stretch becomes one unending, unrelenting series of rapids. At this new pace, there is no opportunity to pull over and scout out what's ahead. The focus becomes maneuvering around what is right in front of you, instead of looking downstream at what is coming next.

Even harder, the run becomes unpredictable and there is no way to see what kind of obstacles are under the surface—which is exactly what had landed me in this situation, separated from my kayak and paddle, straddling rocks, and attempting to stay afloat as the river roared on.

As I stood there, stuck in an impossible position, I questioned everything that had led me to that moment. I had known before entering the river that, ironically, although the water was churning down the river at a rapid pace, it would take me twice as long as it usually did to paddle the same distance. I had known it was likely that I would get stuck on submerged rocks, tangled in trees that had fallen into the river, or dumped into the water because of the runoff. But I believed my expert paddling skills would keep me out of the situation I found myself in: tipped out of the kayak and watching my paddle float away.

The unfortunate truth was that, even though I was a skilled paddler, it didn't matter. The flooding river diminished my performance, made it harder to navigate obstacles, and caused me to move at a much slower pace—even though the water itself was moving faster than usual.

Organizations Are Like Rivers

Flow   Flood

SIMILAR TO MY FAVORITE WHITE-WATER river, organizations experience various states of *flow* and *flood*.

When an organization is flowing like it should, things just seem to work right—people work hard, actually deliver great things with ease, and love their work. Innovative ideas emerge and transform into real value. Collaboration feels like second nature, and accomplishments pile up.

But in a state of flood, the work is too fast, too much, and most things take longer to finish than anyone expects. There is no limit to the amount of work that gets started, and an unlimited amount never gets finished. Flooding in organizations is what makes people feel like they're caught in a wild frenzy of activity, overwhelmed, barely in control, and not getting enough work done.

Simply put, flood is the feeling of working hard while drowning in hard work.

It probably won't surprise you to learn that most organizations are flooding. Some are aware of it, but most become oblivious to it because a raging river *feels* like it's moving fast. The water may be moving fast, but *you* are moving slow.

Fast water does not mean fast travel. Chaos can be easily mistaken for the feeling of productivity when we are in a constant state of urgency. This happens especially when our entire culture of *modern management*—a term that encompasses the organizational management practices of our time that are extremely common but out of sync with reality—reinforces the illusion that working hard equals being productive.

In other words, it doesn't matter how great of a paddler I am. If I'm swept up in a flooded river, I'm going to spend more time managing its mayhem and hurdles and less time moving toward my destination.

But there are even bigger tolls that a flooding river creates beyond productivity issues. In flooding organizations, leaders put people in positions where they are forced to choose between doing great work and prioritizing their own well-being. And in addition to the very real human cost, flooding organizations waste time and energy managing the flood instead of doing the actual work that matters most.

As an expert in organizational learning and change, I teach leaders how to solve problems and adapt fast with high-performing teams. I have spent nearly two decades consulting with organizations across diverse sectors—from nonprofits to universities to global Fortune 50 companies—and the patterns and connections I find between organizational multitasking, burnout, and performance are undeniable.

It should come as no surprise that flooding within an organization, can cause some serious damage—just as it did to my kayak, paddle, and pride. Economist and father of lean thinking, W. Edwards Deming, calls these "heavy losses,"[1] by which he means losses of immeasurable cost that fundamentally harm the DNA of an organization.

There are three critical heavy losses that I witness happening over and over again in organizations:

1. **People burn out.** Burnout is more likely when employees are trying to navigate a flooding river indefinitely. The result? People are overworked, exhausted, and discouraged. People who are experiencing chronic burnout either disengage or leave.

2. **Innovation evaporates.** Innovation requires learning, experimenting, and providing the space for creative thinking. In other words, it's hard to dream up new paddle designs when you are navigating a rushing, flooding river and trying to fish for your dinner at the same time.

3. **Time and energy are wasted on solving the wrong problems.** The biggest loss of all is when people lose precious time and energy trying to solve the wrong problems. It usually plays out something like this:

   The Problem: *Workload is becoming unsustainable and employee turnover is becoming more frequent, so you focus on building morale.*

The Solution: *Let's add frozen yogurt in the lobby and do team-building days!*

Or...

The Problem: *Everyone is overwhelmed and working too hard.*

The Solution: *Let's tell everyone they have to use all of their personal time off days before the year ends (but they'll still need to get all of the same work done).*

When leaders only address the symptoms they see, they believe they're taking action, but in reality, they have only added more to their infinite to-do lists and exerted more energy. Unless you dig deeper and make an effort to truly understand the underlying patterns, you will get trapped in an endless cycle of chasing fixes that solve the wrong problems.

Organizational flooding is the leading killer of high performance everywhere.

Based on my research, there are three primary factors that are always at play in organizations flooded with competing priorities:

1. The silent pressure to do it all

2. The reality that change is constant and unpredictable

3. The fetishization of output

At least one of these factors, usually all three, are the primary enablers of flooding in every organization that I have ever worked with.

The Silent Pressure to Do It All

THE PRESSURE WE EXPERIENCE FROM ourselves and others to do exceptional work isn't inherently bad. But the pressure to *do it all* is an entirely different beast.

We've all experienced the intense pressure to do everything at once at some point in our lives, but most leaders feel this pressure all the time. I have a high amount of empathy for those in this situation; the pressure is real, and because leaders face an abundance of important things that need to be addressed, prioritizing becomes seemingly impossible.

Even when leaders are keenly aware of the need to prioritize and know that they *should* say no to some things, it still feels impossibly hard—like the only way to get all of that important work done is to get started on it right away. The reality is that you can say no to 1,000 things, but if you are left with more to do than you have the capacity to accomplish, you will still experience the intense pressure to start it all at the same time.

There is another reality that is equally true. When organizations pursue multiple competing priorities at the same time, heavy losses start to emerge:

1. Quality starts to suffer.

2. People start to suffer.

3. The amazing outcomes you know are possible are harder to come by.

From an individual perspective, this phenomenon of doing multiple things at the same time is well researched, and we've come to know it as multitasking. But what happens when you have a group of people or groups of groups trying to simultaneously deliver on multiple competing objectives at the same time in one organization?

Some call that organizational multitasking; some call it divided focus.

I call it *flooding*. It's the raging, flooding river of competing priorities that takes over and threatens to sweep everyone away with it.

After I told my friend about my ideas for this book, he turned to me and said, "Brandi, I don't know anyone who is as passionate about organizational multitasking as you are. Why do you care so much about it?"

I told him about a conversation I had with a data analyst, Susana, several years ago. Susana worked in a biotech lab that was researching treatments for dementia. I was there at the invitation of the chief people officer to do an assessment on team performance across the company. Susana had been at the company for almost 10 years and was widely viewed as one of the company's most capable analysts. She had been recently assigned to a second lab team that had experienced an unusual amount of turnover and needed someone to fill in. She had many insights to share, including that her to-do list grew longer every day, even though she regularly worked 60+ hours a week.

"We are making some incredible breakthroughs in our research. Exhaustion is just the price to pay for being at the top of my game," she declared. But just a few minutes later, she told me that she was considering accepting a job at a different company because she wasn't sure how much longer she could sustain her pace of work.

That is the moment the idea for this book was sparked.

What would Susana be capable of, I wondered, if she wasn't constantly working under the pressure of spreading her time meeting the needs of two demanding teams?

Too often people are put into situations where they must choose between doing good, important work and prioritizing their own humanity. This is almost always a false choice.

And it leaves employees having to make a hard decision: continue to work for the organization or leave to find a workplace that will be mindful of their well-being and support it in a sustainable way. Happy, healthy people are not a pleasant side effect of a high-performing organization; happy, healthy people are the only path to sustainable high performance.

Change Is Constant and Unpredictable

CHANGE HAPPENS FASTER NOW THAN ever before. Humans and communities are more complex than they have ever been, which means that change inevitably happens in surprising and unpredictable ways.

The reality that change is constant and unpredictable is not the problem. It's just reality. The problems emerge when organizations and their leaders believe that this reality doesn't apply to them. This problem is rooted in the fact that, while there has never really been a monolithic cultural experience, many books on organizational leadership and management collectively assumed there has been. Almost a quarter of the way into the twenty-first century, we know there is not a homogeneous cultural experience, but many organizational structures and practices haven't kept pace because leaders and teams are flooded with a crisis of organizational multitasking.

Modern management practices in the Western world were developed and evangelized almost entirely by white, heterosexual men like Fred Taylor, Peter Drucker, and Jack Welch (with notable exceptions, like Margaret Wheatley and Taiichi Ohno), while big management consulting firms preached the corporate gospel that the greatest social good a company can do is to maximize short-term shareholder profits.[2] The social sector was shaped by this thinking too. In many nonprofits and government organizations, short-term gain is often prioritized over long-term benefit.

Although many people rejected these ideas at the time, and I have met very few leaders who would explicitly embrace the modern management model now, misguided notions about performance and how to manage it still infiltrate many organizations. Too often, we treat organizations like machines and long for the predictability and control that modern management promises. And yet, we are divided all the while from the simple truth that organizations are made of people—people who have evolved to solve problems in very specific and effective ways that do not include multitasking.

With all of this in mind, organizational leaders find themselves at a crossroads: they are habitually perpetuating methods of modern management because of the pressure to do it all, while simultaneously recognizing that these ideas don't work well in a time where change is constant and fast.

A Fetish for Output

MOST OF US ARE STEEPED in the belief that being a high-performer means doing more, all at once. That mindset leads us to erroneously believe that while some people need focus to work, those of us who are really winning can multitask our way through. I have seen this belief manifest time and time again when I have worked with leaders across sectors.

Being labeled as a great multitasker can feel like getting a badge of honor.

If you relate to feeling that way, there is no shame in admitting that you have this mindset. In fact, realizing that you are influenced by this mindset is an important first step in seeing the flood of organizational multitasking.

In 2018, researchers at the University of Michigan gave test subjects a list of tasks to complete and varied whether multitasking was required to complete them. They found that those who were asked to multitask perceived the tasks as more important than those who were not told to multitask. In some cases, multitasking participants outperformed the single-task participants—not because they were working faster, but because the *belief that the work that required multitasking was important* enabled a short-term burst of energy.[3]

We as a Western society attach great value to being busy, and we conflate being busy with being important. Our culture tells us that productivity is about how much we do, but there's a big difference between *output*—the quantity of the work—and *outcome*—the results of the work.

I have zero doubt that you value being a great leader. I'm sure you've read many leadership books and listened to many leadership podcasts and that you care deeply about leading well. You wouldn't pick up this book if you didn't care about your leadership. However, the cognitive illusions and organizational culture that get us into the flood of multitasking are powerful. Whether you embrace it or not, you are steeped in a productivity culture that has a fetish for output.

That is getting in your way of better performance.

Are You Stuck in the Flood?

YOU CAN BE AN EXPERT paddler and still struggle in a raging river.

You can be a good leader and still struggle in a flooding organization.

Since it's not easy to recognize the difference between flow and flood—especially when we've been working in flooding organizations most of our lives—below are some telling and common indicators of the problem. Are any of these common occurrences in your organization?

→ You can get everyone into a meeting because you're the boss. Yet for everyone else, scheduling is impossible; it takes two weeks for them to schedule a half-hour conversation, and the chances are high that some key people will be missing.

→ You can't slow down enough to collaborate for half a day, so you settle for an hour every other week.

→ Too many people on the front lines of your organization struggle to connect their work to progress on your big strategic goals.

→ You find yourself thinking, "Everything feels out of control. If only we had a process that everyone had to follow to get things done."

→ Your primary form of communication is email because you don't have time to communicate in any other, more effective way. "This problem is so important that we can't wait to meet in person about it, so we had better send some emails" is common thinking.

→ Documents are used as a replacement for conversation. Important decisions and interactions are reduced to document dumps: "It's all there. Let me know if you have questions."

→ You've had a headache for the past 10 years. (An executive I worked with actually told me this.)

→ You spend all your days in meetings about work, but you never get around to doing the actual work.

→ You measure success based on how well reality follows your plan instead of how well you adapt your plan as you learn more about reality.

→ You suspect that the data you're looking at doesn't tell the real story, but you go through the motions anyway.

→ Everything is green and on track until it's flaming red and a crisis; nobody feels comfortable saying that things aren't going well until it's too late. Then the finger-pointing begins.

→ Nobody ever disagrees out loud, but the implementation reveals that no one was on the same page to begin with.

Are any of these scenarios familiar?

If so, then that's a clear sign you're in an organization that is flooding.

When leaders are in the middle of an organizational flood, everything seems like a number one priority, and the overload causes back-to-back crises. For that reason, leaders in a flood tend to stick with management techniques that are supposed to work because it seems like there's no time to try a different approach, or that there's too much at stake for experiments.

Rest assured, it is possible to stop the flood. The path forward is simple and pragmatic. The rest of this book will show you how.

Finding a Flow That Is Based in Reality

THIS IS A BOOK ABOUT performance. But it's also a book about people.

I deeply believe—and have seen over and over again—that it's only possible to achieve and *sustain* exceptional high performance through happy, healthy people working together. That is why I wrote this book.

After you read this book, three things are going to happen:

1. You're going to be more productive than you thought you could ever be. So will your teams.

2. You will break the devastating cycle of burnout that affects you and others.

3. Organizational problems that currently seem intractable will become easier to solve.

But wait!

Before you start feeling anxious that I'm going to tell you the solution will be through more company-wide yoga and meditation, know that I believe that's the same idea as wearing a life jacket in a raging river; it may help, but it won't keep the boat from capsizing.

While the key to controlling the flow is simple in theory, it is difficult in practice for one simple reason: it has to be based in reality. You can raise your expectations on performance, and you can do all of this with happy, high-performing teams, but only if you do it all in reality.

Reality isn't convenient, and it's definitely messy. But it also happens to be the only place where good work happens. It's much easier to work within the constraints of human evolution and the laws of physics than it is to change them.

The chapters that follow will be an honest discussion about working in reality, delivering more value, reaching higher performance, and realizing that, at the end of the day, our humanity isn't a liability but the future of all good work.

We will also cover the most effective way to innovate and deliver out-of-this-world value. Spoiler alert: it's through teams who are deeply engaged, focused, and happy. I'll teach you the principles of flow that will allow you to stop the flood and create the environment those teams need to perform.

At the same time, this isn't a "work-life balance, self-care, feel good" sort of book. I'm not going to tell you that you need to lower your expectations. Nor am I going to tell you to do less or sacrifice quality. There are no meditation exercises in these pages.

For now, the biggest thing I want you to understand is this: you do not have to choose between high performance and happy people. You couldn't choose even if you wanted to—because you'll never achieve the performance your organization is capable of without teams of happy people. It is possible, and necessary, for you and everyone in your organization to embrace well-being in order to reach the highest levels of performance that your organization is capable of.

Shape the River

AS A LEADER, IT IS your job to shape your organization to enable the flow of good work and value.

The good news is that, while riverbeds take thousands of years to evolve and transform, organizations are much more malleable!

This book is your guide to defining the river that is your organization, measuring productivity by how the work flows, and ensuring that people are happy, healthy, and deeply engaged in delivering more of the outcomes that matter most.

But before we can continue, we must agree on one thing: a very small step in the right direction is still a step in the right direction.

You may read this book and think you've found the holy grail to solving all your problems. Alternatively, you may read it and think none of it will work in your organization. I'd encourage you to take a third approach—to view it as a better step on your road of improvement.

It's time to shape your river.

CHAPTER TWO

THE INCONVENIENT TRUTH ABOUT HUMANS

LET'S GO THROUGH A LITTLE mind experiment together.

Imagine that I, your manager, give you, the employee, a pitcher of water and ask you to take it from point A to point B in a room. It's very important that you accomplish the goal, but quality matters too, so you can't spill a drop. Oh, and of course, we're on a deadline, so you need to get it there as fast as possible.

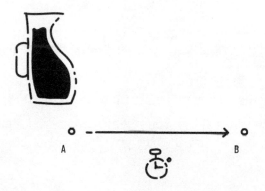

You complete the task well; it's a little challenging, but not that hard, right?

Now imagine that I take that same pitcher of water and pour the water into four cups, each one full to the brim. I need you to walk those four full cups of water across the room, using only your two hands to carry them. The deadline is fast approaching, so speed is important here, but still, you can't spill anything. Quality is just as important as it was before, but you need to go as fast as you can. You'll have to figure out how to juggle both while literally juggling sloshing cups.

It's fundamentally the same thing you did before—you're moving an equivalent amount of water across the room—and because you did so well with the pitcher project, I know I can count on you to successfully move the cups.

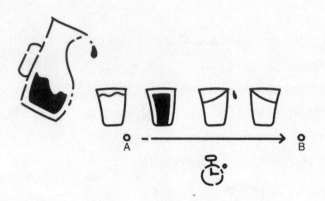

And yet, this task does *not* feel the same. In fact, it's not the same at all.

What seems like an equivalent job on paper suddenly becomes more difficult in real life. You might manage to juggle those cups across the room, but it's going to be a lot harder. You will move more slowly, and the risk of losing some water is greater.

Now, imagine that you successfully transported those cups from point A to point B. I'm pleased because you did a great job on the project—in fact, I'm so confident in your abilities that I want you to take on a great new creative project I have in mind.

I know what your capacity is and don't want to overwhelm you, so I'm going to give you the same amount of water. But the catch this time is that you have to carry three cups and one strangely shaped vase.

At this point, your job is going to get harder no matter how good of a water carrier you are. You might spill some water, and, without exception, the speed and quality of your performance will decrease. Internally, you might feel trapped, be stressed, and get disappointed in yourself for failing to carry the water like you used to.

As your manager, I understandably become frustrated and confused by this change. I then might ask you, "Why is your performance dropping like this? It's the same amount of water and the same amount of distance. What's going on?" I send you an article on time management and hope you figure it out.

The Peculiar Math of Capacity Management

YOU CAN SEE THE PROBLEM here: I'm asking you to do the same task, *sort of*, but the work is completely different. Your capacity to carry the water has changed. There is no good way to juggle water in multiple containers across a room with just your hands.

In organizations, this trick of dividing time and energy is called *capacity management.*

You might be tasked with one project that's meant to take up 20% of your capacity, one that's meant to take up 60%, another that's supposed to take up 5%, and a final one that should take up 15%.

Theoretically, you're fine. The numbers add up to 100%. You're at capacity and should be able to do the work easily.

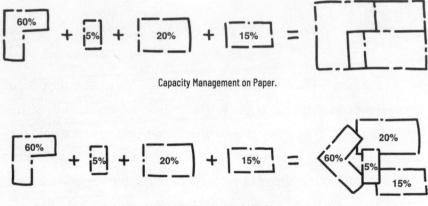

Capacity Management on Paper.

Capacity Management in Reality.

And yet, while the math works out on paper, it never adds up in real life.

Instead of being able to do the work easily, you are overworked and scrambling to keep up. This may cause you to internalize doubt that perhaps you aren't the high-performer you believed yourself to be or to think that you are doing something "wrong," which isn't true.

The reason people in your organization are struggling is because carrying a bunch of cups doesn't equate to carrying a pitcher—regardless of water volume. In other words, the whole is greater than the sum of its parts, and not in a good way.

It's easy to see how this plays out with physical tasks: most of us have two hands and can easily carry two cups of water. However, all of us will start to struggle when the number of cups exceeds our number of hands.

But when shifting into the realm of cognitive work, that tangible limit seems to disappear.

There are still limits, but they aren't visible—unlike the physical limit of only having two hands.

Even though it doesn't actually work, many of us have a tendency to apply this kind of capacity management because it seems like we ought to be able to divide our time into fractions that we use to get different types of work done. It feels like we *can* multitask, so we attempt it all the time. The reality is that the human brain can't be divided into percentages and parts. Our brains just don't work that way.

We'll spend this chapter unpacking how human brains *do* work to explain in a more visceral way how and why multitasking is so costly. Let's start with the fallacy that is multitasking.

Researchers at the Vanderbilt Center for Integrative and Cognitive Neuroscience performed functional brain scans on thousands of people, observing their brain activity while they performed a wide variety of cognitive tasks. Their conclusion: "Despite the impressive complexity and processing power of the human brain, it exhibits severe capacity limits in information processing. Nowhere is this better illustrated than when we attempt to perform two tasks at once."[4]

The brain can perceive multiple sensations at the same time, and it can complete life-sustaining activities (breathing, digesting food, etc.) while engaging in other activities, but it cannot perform two conscious tasks, such as reading emails and participating in a planning meeting, at the exact same time.[5]

At this point, you may be thinking, "I do that all the time." And it may be true that you regularly catch up on emails during meetings, especially if you are meeting remotely. However, your focus is fractured, not equally divided.

Fractured moments of focus add up to major costs, costs like the ones we discussed last chapter (employee burnout and wasted time spent solving the wrong problems) and negative collective consequences like lower-quality work, lack of equity, and ineffective collaboration.

These losses multiply as one person turns into a team and as teams turn into an entire organization. And when you have a large group of people trying to juggle water in a bunch of cups and vases, the spilling starts to add up.

Suddenly, there's a flood on your hands.

Thankfully, the flood can be reversed. As we will discuss in Chapters 5 and 6, the solution will come from a practice that is well-established as the antidote to flooding, but not widely applied across most organizations: *flow principles*. Flow principles will not require you or your organization to do less. They will actually enable you to accomplish more, but differently.

If you're ever going to be able to implement flow principles, there are two truths you must commit to navigating as a leader. If you don't accept these realities, you likely won't be able to take any of the actions I recommend in this book.

1. Human brains, including yours, work in some very specific, predictable, and powerful ways when it comes to performance and productivity. This is the focus of the current chapter.

2. Groups of humans perform their best and are happiest under some very specific and predictable conditions. We'll dive into those conditions in Chapter 4.

These truths are inconvenient because they push against modern management's beliefs about what it means to be a high-performer and how to lead a high-performing organization. However inconvenient they may be, they are still true.

Human Brains and Their Executive Functions

YOUR BRAIN, ALONG WITH EVERY other human brain, evolved to work as a whole, not as a slice of the larger pie. Your brain is therefore well-equipped to solve one whole problem in a particular moment, not slices of many problems simultaneously.[6]

Almost five decades of research into cognitive science shows that we have built into our DNA very definite capacities when it comes to how we're able to work. When we understand and work with our DNA and not against it, more is possible.

Humans have evolved a complex set of skills and processes that enable us to respond to change, work together, and solve problems. These are called *executive functioning skills*, and understanding them is the key to getting more work done effectively. Governed by the frontal cortex of the brain, executive functions are a variety of cognitive, self-management, and collaboration skills that people use to solve problems.[7]

Executive functioning is kind of what it sounds like: the executive management of our brains. These functions make it possible for us to play around with new ideas, change our mindsets, explore creative ways to solve problems, think before acting, manage communication, respond to unanticipated challenges, and focus.[8]

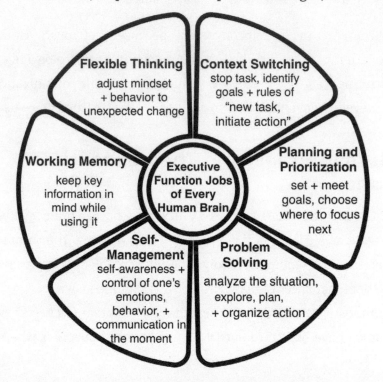

Flexible Thinking
adjust mindset + behavior to unexpected change

Context Switching
stop task, identify goals + rules of "new task, initiate action"

Working Memory
keep key information in mind while using it

Executive Function Jobs of Every Human Brain

Planning and Prioritization
set + meet goals, choose where to focus next

Self-Management
self-awareness + control of one's emotions, behavior, + communication in the moment

Problem Solving
analyze the situation, explore, plan, + organize action

Back to how your brain solves problems. Your brain and mine perform executive functions one at a time. However, the challenge is that problems, tasks, and ideas rarely come at us single file, one at a time. Our human brains have developed specialized skills to manage this.

Two of the most frequently used executive functions are *goal shifting* and *rule activation*, commonly known in tandem as *context switching.*[9] When we are in a situation where we need to tackle more than one thing at a time, we use these skills to switch back and forth between the tasks we are trying to accomplish.

Goal shifting is the process of changing your focus from one activity to another. An example would be switching from reviewing the next quarter's marketing plan to collaborating on a new-hire recruitment project. Immediately, the brain reorients itself, identifies the goal of the new task, and moves on to rule activation.

Rule activation is the process of implementing the new set of "rules" for engagement. For example, the social rules are different when I am meeting one-on-one with a leader who I've been coaching for months versus when I am facilitating a prioritization session with the executive team of a company I just started working with last week. My brain must rapidly assess any changes in people or circumstance, recall the rules for engaging or completing the task, apply those rules to the new goal, and then get to work.

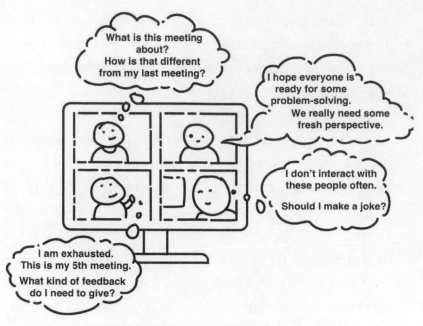

Goal Shifting and Rule Activation are always the first two executive
functions that we must perform.

The executive functioning capacity of our brains evolved to collaborate, solve seemingly intractable problems, and innovate in powerful ways. But it does this by enabling only *one* executive functioning task at a time.

This is called the *bottleneck phenomenon*, a principle that states that the frontal cortex of your brain can only perform one executive functioning task at a time.[10]

Numerous brain-scan experiments show that if more than one task is presented—for example, drawing a shape, saying your phone number, and choosing which snack you want—your brain will form a queue for the tasks.

The drawback to the bottleneck phenomenon is that there is a cognitive load associated with managing that queue. You will perform each task more slowly if you are managing a queue of executive function tasks than you would have if you were doing them independently. The longer the queue, the greater the cognitive load. The length of time it takes to do each task increases every time something is added to your list. If you're trying to accomplish two tasks at once, you will spend about 40% of your time and energy context switching, leaving only 60% brainpower to actually complete those tasks.[11]

The bottleneck phenomenon also applies to more advanced skills.

For example, because of the way the bottleneck phenomenon works, it's impossible to think about what you are going to discuss in your next meeting and make sense of new information being shared in your current meeting at the same time. You can switch between these two tasks very quickly, and it may *feel* like you are accomplishing both activities simultaneously. But in reality, you can only do one of them at a time.

So, what's going on?

Your brain is rapidly engaged in context switching, which you now know means goal shifting and rule activation. In order to shift from planning what you are going to discuss next (communication management) to making sense of the current presentation (analysis), your brain quickly recalls the purpose of the presentation (goal shifting) and applies the social norms that apply (rule activation).

Any time something shifts in a conversation or environment, your brain immediately goes into goal-shifting, then rule-activation mode. Your brain cycles through these executive functions over and over again in response to the changing circumstances.

What we want our brains to do.

What we think our brains do.

What our brains actually do.

Unfortunately, we can't opt out of these brain activities or change them to be more favorable to settings that force multitasking.

So, what does this all mean?

That it's easier to work with the evolution of our brains than to work against it. There is a physiological and cognitive reason why we can't juggle so many different things at once, even though it seems like we should be able to.

The Reason You Are Tired and Flooding

LET'S RETURN TO THE RIVER.

This time, instead of being in a kayak, we have a big boat. The twist is, you aren't responsible for managing just your boat—but also the five other boats traveling down the river with you. All of them have different crews and different goals and are moving at different speeds.

You are hopping back and forth from boat to boat, making sure that each one is heading in the right direction and that everyone has what they need. You are the fleet's admiral, responsible for ensuring the high performance and function of every boat.

Every time you jump into a new boat, your brain must perform its two mandatory executive functions:

1. When **goal shifting**, you must recall the purpose of the boat (Fishing? Scouting out a new route? Collecting data samples?) and why, in this particular moment, you are in the boat (An update on progress? Identifying key metrics? Reviewing a new prototype?).

2. When **rule activating**, you must assess the people in the boat and the rules of engagement (Is the boat captain someone you've worked with for years or your most recent hire? Does the crew get along? What language do they speak? What kind of boat are they in? And how is all of this different from the last boat you were on?).

Now that you've made it into the boat and have familiarized yourself with its goals and rules, you're ready to tackle the questions that brought you to the boat in the first place. The only problem now is that you're almost out of time.

In an organization, this is what happens when you are in back-to-back meetings all day or trying to simultaneously manage five projects. It's what happens when you spend most of a 30-minute meeting with a team getting everyone up to speed before being able to move on to what the meeting was supposed to be about—with what little time you have left.

Goal shifting and rule activation are two of the most demanding executive functions, and the more complex the activity, the more time it takes for your brain to perform that activity.[12] And it can take *a lot* more time. A study in the 2013 *Annual Review of Psychology* found that it takes up to 10 times longer to successfully complete a new task when the goal and the rules change at the same time.[13]

It turns out that as you were hopping between boats, you were spending the majority of your energy and time on goal shifting and rule activation.

In the real world, if you're splitting your attention between two activities or projects, you will be spending 60% of your time and energy doing the work and 40% of your time goal shifting and rule activating. Take it up one notch to three projects, and you get just 40% of your brainpower to do the work, while you spend up to 60% of your time and energy just managing the work of switching back and forth between tasks.[14] That time and energy is spent in moments and milliseconds throughout your day; it slips away almost entirely under the radar of your cognitive awareness.

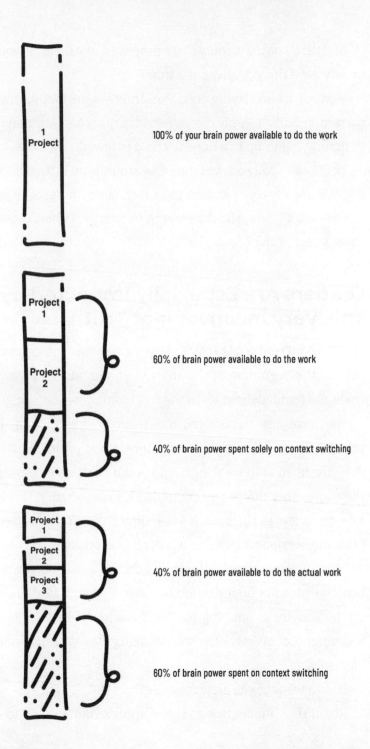

And that's based on only three projects. How dreamy would it be to only have three projects at a time?

Most of us are trying to make progress on many, many important tasks in a single day, week, and month. All of that context switching tallies up to a huge tax paid in energy and time.

This is why you and everyone else around you is tired and flooding. We are simply spending too much time and energy jumping in and out of boats, all while trying to navigate them successfully down a raging river.

Leaders Are Especially Impacted by This Very Inconvenient Truth

LET'S SAY THAT YOU HAVE deeply embraced the art of delegation. At the beginning of the quarter, you identified your top five goals and handed them off to the five teams you manage.

You have just empowered five teams to pursue your highest priorities in addition to their ongoing highest priorities. Now your days are filled with meetings about each of these goals, on top of the many other things you get pulled into as a leader. You go from one-on-one meetings with your direct reports to reviews and planning sessions all day, all week, all quarter long.

This means you are jumping back and forth between all the boats within your organization but spending your best brainpower on the activity of jumping back and forth and very little time on meaningful conversations, sensemaking, collaboration, or problem-solving.

It's no wonder you are exhausted!

Recall that human beings spend approximately 40% to 60% of

their work time context switching in most organizations.[15] Think about the math on that. That means that for every million dollars you spend on payroll every year, as much as $600,000 of it is spent on paying people to switch from one thing to another. How much value does switching back and forth add to your organization?

Before you start to dismiss this as not applying to you or your team of high-performing multitaskers, there is compelling evidence that people's perception of how well they context switch is not at all correlated with actual ability.[16] Believing you are good at context switching doesn't actually mean you are.

Productivity researchers took a deep-dive look into the effect that individual multitasking has on just the American economy. In 2005, the cost was nearly $650 billion a year. But that was before the era of 24-7 connectivity. Based on inflation alone, in 2022 the cost time lost due to multitasking will soar to over a trillion dollars.[17] And yet, those numbers barely scratch the surface of the heavy losses that are caused by the flood of organizational context switching.

You aren't alone in the struggle—this is a problem facing nearly every organization. You also aren't a bad leader for finding this truth inconvenient. It would, in fact, be much more convenient to plan and accomplish goals if humans could multitask without impact to themselves, to quality, and to outcomes. It would be more convenient, but it's not reality.

The science on multitasking is conclusive and clear, but it doesn't often compel action—it's hard to translate this research into actionable steps that feel doable. I often find that leaders already know that multitasking isn't great for their organizations, but they either can't overcome the inertia of the status quo or believe the costs associated with multitasking are unavoidable. Most of the time, these views are powered by powerful illusions that make it difficult to embrace the reality of how our brains work most effectively.

There are three illusions that every leader encounters at some point. These are like mirages in the desert: they will make you think reality is different than it is. They are specious, having the appearance of being true on the surface, but when they are examined more closely, the logic crumbles. Like most false beliefs, these illusions are powerful because they are comforting.

The Treading Water Illusion

TREADING WATER ISN'T THE SAME as swimming across the channel, but both consume lots of energy. We think we are making progress toward our goal, only to discover we've merely been treading water.

Treading water takes a lot of energy, but it's not the same as swimming across the lake.

In the United States, there are cultural forces propping this illusion up. Ideas about productivity, efficiency, and laziness have us trying to bend reality. The ethic of hard work has resulted in a fetish for output and doing more while accomplishing less.

If I am working hard, I am doing important things.

If I am busy, I am important.

If I am producing, I have value.

At least, that is what the illusion encourages us to believe.

In a collaborative study, researchers at Columbia, Georgetown, and Harvard found that busyness is a uniquely American signal for perceived status, social value, and economic worth. After analyzing thousands of social media posts and marketing ads, they concluded in the *Journal of Consumer Research*: "long hours of work and lack of leisure time have become a powerful status symbol."[18]

These same researchers found that, when given information about the accomplishments and successes of fictitious people, study participants estimated that extremely successful people worked more hours and took fewer vacation days than those who had less notable achievements. They also found that these perceptions were highly consistent among American participants, but that European participants did not correlate busyness with success in the same way.[19] We too often settle for treading water when the same effort, or even less, is required to swim forward.

The Fancy Boat Illusion

"BUT THERE ARE SO MANY important things to do," you might say.

Yes, this is true. The truth of this is going to make you want to bend the reality that we've just established. You will be tempted to try to improve your context-switching skills. You might be tempted to purchase fancy software for your company that optimizes project plans and to-do lists. You may want to change your HR screening questions to identify people who are more efficient multitaskers.

Having an abundance of important things to do does not change how your brain works, but it does present a problem. It's inconvenient and sometimes impossibly hard to identify the *most* important things to do. You have likely already winnowed away everything that you deem nonessential. You've said no to dozens, maybe thousands, of ideas already. What you are left with is the important stuff that has to get done.

The dilemma then becomes, How will we get everything that matters done? This is one of the driving questions that every leader I have ever met has wrestled with in some form or another.

When faced with a conundrum like how to get all the important work done, we naturally seek out potential solutions. In this place of high pressure, high stakes, and high performance, we tend to favor more complex solutions over simple ones, even though simple solutions tend to have better outcomes.

It's a well-established cognitive bias, aptly named *complexity bias*. A cognitive bias is a decision-making shortcut that our brains employ in an attempt to solve problems faster.[20]

At one point in our evolutionary history, these biases may have served our human ancestors well, helping them survive. In the twenty-first century, these biases tend to help us solve a short-term problem, with long-term consequences.

It's like identifying that the river is rising, knowing we have too many boats without enough crew in the raging water. Instead of taking a boat out of the water, we start adding embellishments and fancy features to the boats because we believe that if people get fancy boats, they will be more motivated to work harder.

Complexity bias is an avoidance tactic. We put great energy and

Bells and whistles won't get you to your destination.

effort into complicated solutions that are less likely to work, instead of pursuing a simple—but perhaps difficult—solution that will more effectively pull us through to the other side.

Much time and money has been invested to figure out how to make workers better at multitasking. Microsoft has developed AI technology designed to "suggest" small tasks that can be completed in the spare moments between bigger tasks.[21] (Reality check: this only increases our need to context switch, which is the problem in the first place.) The overwhelming conclusion of cognitive scientists is that we'd be better off avoiding scenarios where multitasking is required.

The simple solution here is to shift our paradigm of productivity and high performance toward outcomes (the results of our work) instead of output (how much work we complete), but that kind of change is challenging. The fight-or-flight part of our brains kicks in and complexity bias takes over, convincing us that if we try hard enough, we can fight through problems with fancy equations and more multitasking.

One of the reasons it is so tough to change our approach around multitasking and productivity is that mindset shifting is an executive functioning task. It's hard to do the work of unpacking a well-established mindset when we are constantly engaged in goal shifting and rule activation all the time.

Imagine you are that admiral, jumping back and forth between all those boats moving down the river, trying hard to stay focused on the work and not fall in the fast-moving water. How likely is it that you would slow down to consider the possibility that this armada would function a lot better if each boat had a dedicated captain?

We simply do not have the brain capacity to adopt new mindsets while navigating raging rivers and jumping between boats.

The Saddle a Unicorn Illusion

HAVE YOU EVER TRIED TO put a saddle on a unicorn? No?

You will never be able to put a saddle on a unicorn, because unicorns aren't real.

You can make the most amazing saddle in the world, or write up diagrams and instructions and process manuals, but you still can't put a saddle on a unicorn. The reason? While my four-year-old might disagree, unicorns aren't real.

And neither is modern management's version of capacity management.

Yet many a spreadsheet is created, and a massive amount of energy is spent attempting to answer mythical questions: "What percentage of our capacity are we using? Are we at full utilization? When will this be finished?"

A leader I once worked with calls this "a game of utilization Tetris," in which managers try to maximize the utilization rate of every team, dividing each person's time into smaller and smaller percentages to get the work done. It's not a game this leader recommends.

Complicated formulas are developed, but the math and the logic behind the attempt to manage capacity is just as flawed as trying to put a saddle on a unicorn. I've frustrated many managers with my simple answers to these questions:

Question: *What's our capacity?*

Answer: *It's the number of people on your team.*

Question: *When will this be finished?*

Answer: *It depends. How many other projects are you working on at the same time?*

I once told a manager that we would need someone from his team fully dedicated, 100%, to a strategic initiative. A week later, the manager let me know that while he didn't have one person who could be fully dedicated, his team would be 100% dedicated.

He had an employee in India who could dedicate 50% of her time, another employee in California who could do 30% of his capacity, and one new hire who could offer 20% capacity.

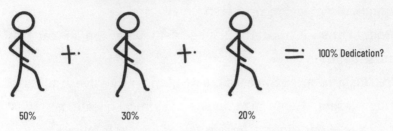

The modern management approach to dedicated team members doesn't add up.

The pressure to get the important work done pushes us to accept some very funny math.

Why You Do This

IN PHYSICAL TASKS, LIKE CARRYING objects, it's easy to see a natural limit on how much we can do at one time. Most of us have two hands, and we can carry two cups of water without risking a spill. The boundary is clear. But as soon as we move into the realm of knowledge work, we can no longer physically see the cognitive work being done—at least, not in the same ways as we can see someone carrying water or kayaking down a river. In that space of not seeing and under the pressure of important work to do, we try out the illusion that we can divide ourselves and conquer.

Capacity cannot be managed and allocated by percentages. We have to accept that each person is whole—we cannot divide people into parts. Humans are not the sum of their parts (any more than a pitcher of water is made up of four smaller cups). They're people. While computers and machines can multitask, our brains cannot be reprogrammed to do the same.

You'll often hear leaders say things like, "How many resources do we need for that?"

When I hear this, I'll frequently ask, "What kind of resources?"

Once, a manager replied to this question, straight-faced, with "human resources," and then proceeded to explain to me how human resources are just one of the inputs into a project they were working on. According to that manager, if they knew how many human resources they needed, they could plan the work for "full resource allocation."

Employees aren't "resources," they're people, and they interact and do work with all the creative possibility and real constraints that all people have. Resource planning and management as a function is common in big companies, but the desire to manage capacity exists even more so at small organizations.

Recently, I was in a coaching session with the CEO of a small data analytics firm in New York. I had just started working with this organization as the COVID-19 pandemic caused massive closures and disruption in the United States. The CEO was working through an emergent strategy for virtual teaming as everyone started to work from home.

As an empathetic leader who was still bound by the spell of the Saddle a Unicorn Illusion, she knew that the unknowns and life-altering changes that were going on would have an impact on people's work. But what she really wanted to know was what percentage of her employees' capacity would be devoted to work versus home life and general overwhelm caused by the pandemic.

On a strategy call, she wondered if she should instruct her managers to plan for 20% less "resource utilization." She wanted to have realistic expectations, but she wanted those expectations to fit neatly into a formula.

People aren't resources. They don't come in parts. And a person's time cannot be neatly divided into percentages without accounting for the cost of context switching. There is no way to quantify what part of each person's executive function capacity would be devoted to home versus work tasks. There is no formula because our brains don't function in percentages of capacity.

Trying to solve the capacity management problem gets us asking the wrong questions and focused on the wrong kind of productivity.

Here's what I told that leader: *Encourage your managers to spend more time defining the goals that you need your team to accomplish and prioritize the order they need to get done.* In other words, figure out which boats are most important to get all the way down the river first. Let go of the formula for capacity management; it's a waste of your time, and you don't have time to waste.

The effort required to divide and allocate percentages of an employee's time has about the same return on investment studying the science of unicorn-saddling techniques.

LEADING IN REALITY

Attention Gremlins

PRIORITIES, FIRES, AND INITIATIVES COME and go. Even after we artfully set priorities and protect our calendars, these little gremlins find their way in, diverting attention, stealing time, and monopolizing our energy. While setting priorities, communicating them, and tracking them helps everyone stay focused, I've learned that there is something even sneakier at play when it comes to stealing my attention.

As leaders, we try to hone our empathetic skills. In part, our job is to understand the experience of our team members so that we can help them thrive and do the best work of their lives. But there is a fine line between understanding their experience and feeling responsible for their experience. When I slip into feeling responsible for my team's experience, I unintentionally take on their priorities because I want to be there for them—and with them. I join them in the arena, as researcher Brené Brown would say. But, by continuously joining them in the arena, I unintentionally undermine their agency and blur the lines between healthy and unhealthy support. When this happens, my attention is diverted.

Finding and holding the boundaries of what you are responsible for is personal work that never seems to be done!

—Anna Love, CEO & Founder, Stoked[22]

You Can Start Taking Action Right Now

ORGANIZATIONAL CHANGE ACTIVIST adrienne maree brown reminds us, "How we are at the small scale is how we are at the large scale."[23] To influence large-scale change, start at the small scale.

All I want you to do right now is to start to pay attention to how many boats you jump in and out of during the day. Perhaps look back at your calendar. On your last workday, how many meetings did you have? On how many topics? Was it more than three? More than seven? More than 10?

Count up how many different initiatives, goals, or projects you are responsible for in a given week. Now, consider that each of those initiatives, goals, projects, and tasks is like a different boat, with its own objective and rules of engagement.

How many boats do you have? Grab a sticky note and write the number down.

Are you surprised at the number? You may be. You may also find that the number of "boats" you manage right now is exactly what you'd expect: a lot.

Most of us would probably not want to be in an actual river and responsible for that number of physical boats, so why force the same number of boats into your head?

And yet that's exactly what we often do. We do that day in, day out for weeks, months, and—for many of us—*years*, and burnout becomes a very real threat.

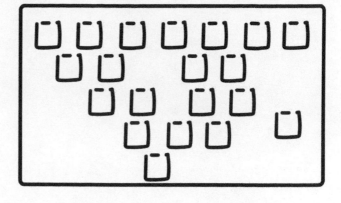

How many mental "boats" are you responsible for?

CHAPTER THREE

THE REAL REASON PEOPLE BURN OUT

IN MAY 2020, TWO CENTRAL Michigan river dams on the Tittabawassee River failed, releasing enough water to fill an Olympic-sized swimming pool every two seconds. It went on like this for days, creating a raging flood that overwhelmed everything and everyone in its path.[24] Thousands of residents were forced to evacuate, homes were destroyed, and entire towns were replaced with deep rushing water.

People were flooded out of their homes and neighborhoods for weeks due to the torrential rain, the dams that were too easily overcome, and the proximity of homes and businesses to the river.

No single individual could have done anything on their own to stop the flood. It wasn't an individual problem—it was an ecosystem problem.

The same is true of burnout.

Trying to reduce the damage of burnout with individual strategies is like telling the people near the Tittabawassee River to stockpile sandbags and work on their self-rescue plans for the next time the dam fails. Sandbags might keep the flood at bay for a while, but they will never address the core problem. And people should not have to constantly be updating a self-rescue plan—for floods or for work.

It would be far better to design a dam that is equipped for torrential rains than to rely on individuals to flood-proof their homes.

Burnout Is an Ecosystem Problem

BURNOUT IS ONE OF THE most harmful problems facing the modern world of work—so much so that an entire industry has grown around treating it. Researchers, big consulting firms, and organizations all over the globe are keen to identify secrets that stop burnout and offer their solutions. The World Health Organization has identified burnout as a public health crisis and defines it as follows: "Burn-out is a syndrome conceptualized as resulting from chronic workplace stress that has not been successfully managed. It is characterized by three dimensions:

→ feelings of energy depletion or exhaustion;

→ increased mental distance from one's job, or feelings of negativism or cynicism related to one's job; and

→ reduced professional efficacy."[25]

In 2017, the time-tracking company Kronos asked over 600 human resource executives what they saw as the biggest threats to their effectiveness. About 95% acknowledged that employee burnout is sabotaging workforce retention, and 87% named improving retention as a high priority.[26]

In this same study, employees of those companies were interviewed. Employees reported that an unreasonable workload and too much after-hours work were two of the top three reasons they were burned out and leaving.[27] A global pandemic that dramatically shifted the world of work has only intensified these challenges, making the stressors of long work hours and increased demands "persistent and indefinite" according to a 2022 Trends Report by the American Psychological Association.[28]

A 2018 version of the same Kronos study found that one out of five HR leaders said they were not planning to address employee turnover because of competing priorities, like new-hire recruitment. The authors of the study concluded, "There is no obvious solution [to burnout] on the horizon."[29]

My response to these HR leaders is a resounding, *Are you kidding me?* How is it that some of the greatest minds in the world are working on solving this problem, and the best they can come up with is a shrug?

You may have experienced this shrug on a smaller level in your own organization. Leaders don't want people to burn out, but the prevailing conclusion seems to be that it's inevitable and mostly outside of our control. The thinking goes that burnout happens to individuals and, therefore, it's a problem that individuals must fix for themselves.

The most archaic organizations consider burnout to be part of the cost of doing business, where people are essentially treated as a non-renewable resource and quitting is seen as an inevitability. In these organizations, people are hired, burned through, and then replaced by hiring fresh resources in the next cycle.

A less archaic—but still problematic—approach is to put the onus of solving a burnout problem on the shoulders of the employees by instructing them to follow a one-size-fits-all template of sorts: Find a better work-life balance. Turn your computer off after hours. Do more self-care. Work flexible hours. Take a wellness day. This response, while more compassionate, is equally flawed and ineffective.

Still, some believe that burnout is something that only happens to the weak or unfocused. Well-intentioned but misguided managers seek out those magical unicorns who appear to burn brighter and brighter with each challenge—perpetuating the illusion that if you are a high-performer, there is no such thing as too much work. Perhaps you even feel that you are a magical unicorn yourself, that being exhausted is the inevitable price to pay for achieving greatness.

Overwhelmingly, organizations treat burnout as an individual problem with individual solutions. This is easy to do because we too quickly accept as reality that overwork is the necessary sacrifice of being a high-performer. Recent massive shifts in the labor market hint that employees are no longer buying into that myth, but employers are slower to catch on.

The truth is that burnout is a threat to you and your organization, but it's not an inevitability. In this chapter, we're going to talk about what's really causing it: the flood of organizational multitasking.

You Do Not Have to Lower Your Expectations

THERE IS ANOTHER CHALLENGE THAT makes it difficult to connect the pattern of organizational multitasking and burnout: leaders wind up in a perceived catch-22 when it comes to address-ing burnout. They know it's a problem, but it's hard to imagine reducing burnout without reducing work. And there is always an abundance of important work.

It is as if the relationship between burnout and performance is two ends of a single teeter-totter, where improving one end inher-ently causes harm to the other. And no one wants to accept lower performance.

Some believe that high expectations and high well-being have a negative correlation where improving one means harming the other. This is true in many organizations The result? Performance suffers.

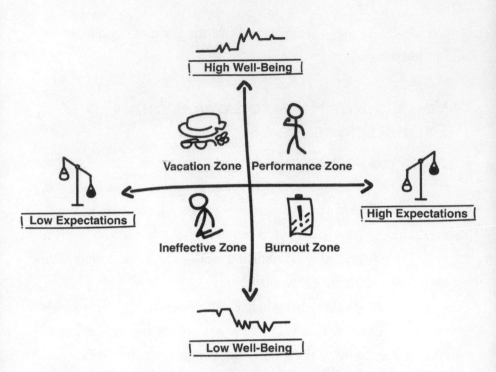

But it doesn't have to be that way. In fact, well-being and high expectations can (and should) have a positive correlation. Well-being **AND** high expectations lead to higher performance.

If employees are overworked and experiencing burnout, then it would make sense that you need to expect less of them, right?

Wrong.

We operate from this misconception because of how we connect self-worth to feeling busy and overworked. If you're in meetings all day, you are important. If you're responding to emails late at night, your opinion must matter. The Treading Water Illusion whispers to us that busyness is a sign of importance, a badge of honor. The cultural fetish for outputs favors quantity. Even if you cognitively disagree, the whispers rarely go away.

As you start to read this chapter, you might begin to worry that I am going to tell you that you will have to expect less from yourself and everyone around you. You might even think I'm going to tell you that in order to stop the flood of organizational multitasking, you'll have to shrink your organizational to-do list, that you'll simply need to do less.

Hand to my heart, doing less is not the remedy. The principles of flow in this book will lead to higher performance, better outcomes, *and* happier people who don't burn out. It's possible, and it's simple, but it's going to require you to lead and make decisions differently. Stopping the flood and starting to flow begins with three practices:

1. Make your work visible.

2. Limit your work in progress.

3. Prioritize.

But before we can get into these practices, you'll have to permanently shift your perspective on your organization in two ways: first, by changing the way you define and value performance in your organization, and second, by adjusting how you view the structure and design of your organization.

We will tackle the former now.

Burnout Causes Employee Turnover, and It's Costing You Lots of Money

If you deal with frequent employee turnover, you are stuck in a never-ending cycle of disruption. You spend too much of your time, energy, money, and capacity for managing change in the process of hiring and onboarding new team members.

Think about how much time it takes to hire someone. You have to write the job description, do the interviews, find the right person, and train them. It then takes weeks or months to get the new hire up to speed and help them develop the institutional knowledge they need in order to do the work. *Then* there is an additional cost because hiring and onboarding adds yet another boat into your already flooding river. You have to boat-jump to train them on top of all your other tasks, which makes everything exponentially harder in terms of creating value and delivering desired outcomes.

Now, consider that it's more costly to replace employees whose primary job requires them to solve problems, think creatively, and work collaboratively. Peter Drucker termed this type of employee a "knowledge worker" and predicted way back in 1966 that knowledge workers would be the driving economic force of the twenty-first century.[30]

In contrast to factory work in the twentieth century, which required workers to perform a task consistently, knowledge work is dynamic, ever-changing, and requires autonomy. This means that when an employee leaves, their unique expertise, experience, and approach to solving problems leaves with them.

It becomes even harder and more expensive to replace managers. The costs of turnover expand quickly. In a sweeping analysis of available research, Gallup estimated that average costs to replace a full-time employee were 50% to 200% of that employee's salary, but the more senior the role, the more expensive hiring can get. For highly skilled workers and senior leaders, the financial cost of replacing an employee can skyrocket to 200% or more of that person's annual salary.[31]

And these are just the *tangible* costs of losing an employee. There is no way to quantify the greater loss of relationships and collaborative skills that lead to more effective team performance.

Consider this reality at scale. Given that most organizations in the United States experienced about 25% of their workforce leaving voluntarily in 2020, the numbers get very scary, very quickly.[32] If you combine this data with the insights from the Kronos report (that many people are leaving jobs because they are burned out), then the costs of employee turnover become exponentially expensive.

Imagine you have a company of 10 highly skilled employees who each make a $100,000 annual salary. On average, two of them will leave every year. You'll spend upward of $200,000 each year on the activities of hiring and training your new employees, and that doesn't even include the actual salary you'll pay. If you have 100 employees, you are more likely paying closer to two million dollars on the costs of turnover each year. And the numbers only go up from there.

But there is another cost of burnout that usually doesn't make it onto the balance sheet: something I call *the flooding tax.*

Because every employee is also conservatively spending 40% of their time on context switching, nearly half of their salary is paying for the thing that is causing overwork and burnout. As the leader of this imaginary company with 10 employees, you are paying an invisible flooding tax of $400,000 every year. And how about the company with 100 employees? The flooding tax could easily be upward of four million dollars every year.

Now imagine this cost if you lead a multinational company with 300,000 employees!

Even if you lead a micro company with just a few employees or your employees make less than those at our hypothetical companies, the flooding tax quickly becomes a staggering percentage of your overall budget.

The amount of money your organization is likely spending on turnover and context switching every year is truly astonishing. Do you know the actual numbers for your organization?

Your Productivity Is Hurt Too

WHEN I STARTED WORKING WITH Patrick, the vice president of digital products at a mid-sized insurance company, his team was experiencing significant turnover. In the six months before I started working with them, about 60% of their team had moved on to other jobs or companies. This was a pattern that had been going on for a few years. Although their work was high priority to the company, the managers and remaining team members were barely working on the product roadmap because they were almost constantly onboarding new hires.

In a problem-solving lab, I asked the entire group to consider what they could have focused on getting done in the previous six months if they hadn't had to onboard so many new team members.

The missed opportunities filled an entire wall.

Economists call these missed opportunities an *opportunity cost*, which is the value of something that is given up in order to obtain something else.[33] The assumption is that this sort of trade-off results in something *more* desirable than the opportunity that was not pursued. In practice, however, desirable, long-term value is often haphazardly traded for the benefit of short-term crisis management.

In Patrick's organization, it was necessary to replace employees; there was no way forward without a full team, but the opportunity cost of all the good work that remained undone was expensive. In this case, opportunity costs were rarely acknowledged and almost never seriously included in decision-making.

Be warned: turnover expenses, flooding tax, and opportunity costs for lost employees aren't the only payments required of an organization overwhelmed by competing priorities. Short-term fixes come with long-term costs. These are the costs that come from solving a problem in a way that fixes the symptom of the problem today but leads to more work down the road. Entrepreneur and author Steve Blank coined a term for this kind of cost: *organizational debt*.[34] Organizational debt takes longer to show up on a balance sheet but is just as costly as technical or financial debt.

In an environment of competing priorities and a culture of organizational multitasking, team members are constantly boat-jumping. In the situation of high turnover, boat-jumping shows up as remaining employees attempting to make progress on multiple priorities *while* supporting new team members or dealing with their own experience of burnout.

It's like teaching a Boating 101 class while simultaneously navigating turbulent white-water rapids.

There is a tremendous amount of waste occurring that is exhausting for everyone. The eventual outcome for organizations stuck in the flood isn't very inspiring: overworked employees stay for years while their engagement goes on autopilot, and because of all the context switching, they underperform. Worst-case scenario, and much more common: employees leave, and you're stuck with the cost of finding new people to do their work.

Employee Turnover Isn't Even the Worst of It

THE HEAVY LOSSES W. EDWARDS DEMING talks about are also what happens when leaders force people to choose between their work and their well-being.[35] Heavy losses are what happens when leaders create situations where people have to make impossible choices. Outcomes diminish and people suffer.

This is one of the greatest tragedies of our modern way of working, and it's even more tragic because it's far from inevitable. I have found that in most organizations, the choice between happiness and doing great work is an unnecessary choice created by leaders who don't understand the real causes of burnout and are likely suffering from the flood of organizational multitasking themselves. There are some jobs that do, in fact, require difficult choices about one's own well-being—for example, working for Doctors Without Borders or UN Peacekeepers. Accepting one of these roles inherently means sacrificing personal safety for the greater good. But most jobs don't actually require one to sacrifice personal safety and well-being to be great at the job.

And yet, the choice between well-being and good work persists. Employees are put into situations where it seems like they have to be drowning in work in order to be high-performers. This false dilemma between doing good work and overworking leads to heavy losses: most people will eventually choose their own well-being over their work and find a different job. Even if they stay in the job, they aren't even able to do their best work because they are overworked and burning out, which is a cost of its own.

Here's What Modern Management Tells You

EVERY LEADER I HAVE EVER met who cares about people hopes to create an environment where people work hard, love their work, and never feel burned out. The desire to do good by your organization and employees isn't the problem here. It's the way modern management operates that traps good leaders into solving burnout the wrong way. Organizations often fall into one of these two very common traps.

Trap #1:
"They Aren't Cut Out for the Job"

WE'VE COVERED IT WELL THUS far: most organizations attempt to address burnout by making it an individual problem. In competitive settings, many adopt the mindset that if a person were truly a high-performer, they wouldn't burn out—and that when certain employees do burn out, that's an inevitability because of their weakness or inherent faults.

It's the equivalent of saying, "Well, if Mary falls into the raging river while jumping between boats, I guess she was never really right for the job to begin with." While this sounds harsh when said out loud, it is the unspoken logic that drives most of our cultural beliefs about burnout and our misguided attempts to address it.

The logic here—that Mary isn't cut out for being a boat captain because she falls into the water when trying to manage multiple boats that are all rushing down a flooded river at the same time—gets in the way of what's most important. If you're in the business of steering high-value boats down a river, then the most important goal is getting the boats to their destination in the most effective way possible. Boat-jumping gets in the way of this goal.

Trap #2:
The Band-Aid Problem

SOME OF YOU PROBABLY READ about that first trap above and thought, "Wow, that's upsetting! I'd never do that." But you are not off the hook just yet. Many leaders are well-intentioned and want to do the right things, but they don't take the right action.

For instance, many leaders think that people get burned out because they aren't taking their personal time off. Some organizations have mandatory minimum time-off requirements, while others try to incentivize people to take time off through "use it or lose it" policies where vacation days are not allowed to accrue from year to year.

Despite these common practices, the number of employees in the United States who don't take all their available paid vacation time increases every year. In 2018, a record-setting 55% of people forfeited paid time off.[36]

Employees aren't burned out because they're not taking their personal days. They're not taking their personal days because they're overworked and feel like they can't. About 54% of Americans report feeling guilty for taking time away from work. Two-thirds of people report planning to work on vacation.[37]

Telling people to take more time off to solve a burnout problem, only to return to work with the same unsolved problems, is like asking a person who is drowning to relax and take a deep breath. It won't actuallyhelp.

Here are some other unhelpful tactics:

→ Volkswagen Management has been known to mandate that email be turned off after a certain point in the evening.[38]

→ Goldman Sachs encourages junior employees to take weekends off. (Ha! Like that is ever going to work if the senior partners are working all weekend. Culture is built by what we see.)[39]

→ A director at a large foundation I once worked with forbade employees from eating lunch at their desks.

The frequency with which one checks email, whether one works weekends, and where one eats lunch are individual actions but not individual problems. Individual actions to combat burnout caused by organizational problems will always be limited to symptom management. Increased paid time off and flexible work schedules are becoming more commonplace as companies attempt to address burnout and prove their great workplace culture.[40] While these actions are commendable, it's not enough.

No amount of vacation, self-care, or team-building activities will be as powerful an antidote to burnout as a leader taking action to stop the flood of organizational multitasking.

Solving the Symptoms of Burnout Doesn't Work

AT THIS POINT, WE'VE DISCUSSED the innumerable ways in which burnout is costly to organizations everywhere. People and organizations have been trying for years to tackle burnout because it is a public health crisis, but most of the time, the problems persist because we go about solving them in the wrong way. Typically, the responsibility for fixing burnout is placed on the individual who is experiencing it. There are countless coaches, books, and workshops all devoted to helping people solve their burnout problems.

But burnout isn't an individual problem any more than a flooding river is an individual problem.

A Gallup survey of 7,500 employees found that five factors were highly correlated with burnout, and that each of these are outside the control of the individual employee:

1. Unmanageable Workload

2. Lack of Role Clarity

3. Lack of Communication and Support from Their Manager

4. Unreasonable Time Pressure

5. Unfair Treatment at Work

Researchers concluded that these five elements are the primary causes of burnout. While these factors explain the reasons why people experience burnout, they are merely the symptoms that show up on the surface, they aren't the underlying cause of the problem.[41] The real issue, which exacerbates every single factor named in the survey, is organizational multitasking.

Like the authors of the Gallup study, I can tell you the reasons why it's hard to paddle down a raging river—the water is moving fast, rocks become hard to see, and the current can sweep you under—but these are not the actual reasons the river is raging.

The river is raging because there is more water flooding the river than the boundaries of the riverbank can handle.

The reasons why people experience unmanageable workload, lack of role clarity, gaps in communication from managers, time pressures, and unfair treatment are almost always influenced by the reality that most of us are flooded with competing priorities and too much work at the same time and, therefore, are spending most of our cognitive and emotional energy context switching *all the time.*

People burn out because leaders think they are asking employees to carry a fixed amount of water across the room, when, in reality, employees are being asked to juggle water in multiple containers that are constantly changing.

It's exhausting. And it gets in the way of doing good work.

The final, but misguided, message for leaders from the authors of the Gallup study is that you can prevent burnout, but only if you change "how you manage and lead your employees." The Gallup authors get it right when they place the responsibility for addressing burnout squarely on organizational leaders. However, viewing burnout through the lens of "what a leader can do to change how employees are managed" still centers burnout as an *individual problem* and not what it really is: an organizational problem.

While burnout is indeed experienced individually, the root cause of it goes back to how the organization (and the work of the organization) is managed, not how individuals are managed—whereas managing burnout by managing employees is an approach that assumes the opposite.

In reality, it's much easier to address burnout by managing the work of the organization through the principles of flow described in the second half of this book than it is to focus on managing the way individuals get their work done.

For everyone in the back of the room: organizational multitasking really does cause burnout.

Reason #1:

Everyone Is Overworked Because They Are Trying to Juggle Water in More Containers Than They Can Physically (or Cognitively) Carry at the Same Time

Given the realities of modern work and the type of work being done, people often get burned out simply because they are overworked. This is even truer for those in high-stress industries (like medicine, law, education, social services, etc.) and for knowledge workers in almost every other industry.

If you're a high-performer who cares about your work but has to spend most of your executive functioning time and energy on managing things that don't add value to the work (i.e., goal shifting and rule activation), then you're going to naturally feel like you are constantly carrying more cups of water than you can hold, spending most of your time ensuring water doesn't spill out. You don't have much time or capacity left to do your actual job.

Reason #2:
Capacity Splitting Adds Social Complexity

Burnout isn't just caused by juggling too many containers at the same time. It's also caused by nearly invisible relational and communication stressors that go along with organizational multitasking.

That is because people aren't *merely* knowledge workers, they are also *highly collaborative* (more on this in Chapter 8). The effectiveness of work hinges on the connections between each person on the team and across the organization, in addition to the knowledge and skills they possess.

Let's say you're a team member with a special skill. You get assigned to support five teams, which seems manageable for you in terms of the work involved. All good, in theory.

But the reality you know by now is that a human can't split their attention into 20% increments and expect to get 100% back, so you start to feel overwhelmed and unable to give your best to any of your projects. That's not a great feeling to have.

What's more, factor in all the new relationships you have to deal with. If you're only on one team with five other people, that's four relationships you have to manage. If you're on five teams with five people per team, it becomes exponentially more complex. You quickly end up with 20 individual relationships and over 100 unique relationship communication pathways to manage.

And it shouldn't come as a surprise that managing communication pathways is an executive function of your brain. You cannot manage communication behaviors at the exact same time you are goal switching or rule activating, which you are doing repeatedly in every exchange.

More People = More Complexity

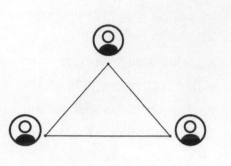

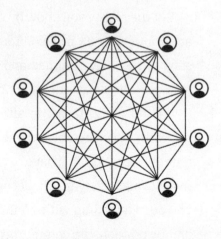

3 people, 3 relationships

5 people, 10 relationships

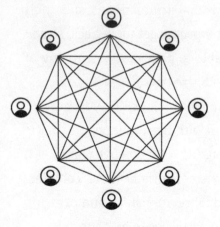

8 people, 28 relationships

10 people, 45 relationships

12 people, 66 relationships   14 people, 91 relationships

Add in the fact that all five teams are likely working on something different: that's five number one priorities and hundreds of opportunities for interruption per day.

Despite your best intentions, you become the bottleneck. This is stressful because you're a team player and you really want to help, but you're constantly juggling priorities, so you feel like you're never giving anyone exactly what they need. You feel like you're disappointing people, and you start to feel progressively worse.

This, my friend, is a very real, mostly invisible, underlying pattern that causes people to experience burnout. And it will never be solved by wellness days, work-life balance, or a flexible schedule.

What does the employee who is experiencing this kind of burnout do next? They start looking for another job. This is the point where I will, very directly and with empathy, say that this problem is *a leadership problem.*

LEADING IN REALITY

The Spirit of the Team

WHAT TYPE OF EMOTIONAL TOLL is doing things the wrong way taking on your team? That harm doesn't show up on a balance sheet, but it has a deep impact on the team.

In a former role, much earlier in my management career, I realized that I was allowing that kind of harm to happen. The spirit of a team can be broken, and I think, as the leader of the team, I saw that our team spirit was broken quite often. And the reason it was broken was because we kept making the team work in ways that felt counterintuitive and making them deal with problems that were entirely solvable. If only we could have stopped stop with the short-term Band-Aids. Teams will give you leeway if something like that is just an industry-wide problem—no one's cracked it—but we had people who would come in and out from different organizations, and they were like, "I know this can be better. I've worked at other places where this is better. And you all are actively choosing not to do it in the best possible way." And that is when the spirit of the team starts to break. I actually had someone tell me, "You're not valuing my time because you're making me do this in an antiquated or incorrect way."

That team had a lot of turnover.

So now I look at the energy and capacity of the team I lead from the perspective of investment, almost like an investment portfolio. Instead of thinking about what the quickest way to fix a problem is, I ask what we can invest now that will lead to a better outcome in the future.

—Senior Manager at Fortune 500 company

Leaders Are Responsible for Stopping the Flood and Preventing Burnout

LEADERS ARE THE SOLE INDIVIDUALS that have the power to stop the flood of competing priorities because they can shape their organizational ecosystems. While it's true that individuals and teams *can* (and do) speak up about being overworked, it takes a lot more courage for them to do so than it would for a leader to proactively make a change.

Good leaders understand that they have a role in addressing burnout and turnover. Many good leaders have equally good intentions. Good leaders know that they must do more than simply address the symptoms of burnout.

But good leaders in flooding organizations are often isolated—with minimal communication or insight into other areas within their organizations—so their solutions only address part of the problem. It happens all of the time. Here are some real ways that I've seen good leaders in flooding organizations attempt to address burnout:

→ Creating a more efficient process and hiring someone to oversee the implementation of that process.

→ Changing up the recruitment strategy to get "more" creative or motivated people.

→ Adding another project manager.

→ Starting an employee engagement program.

→ Planning potlucks to boost morale (glossing over how this adds one more extraneous task to everyone's overflowing to-do list).

If a good leader is only looking at their part of the organization while simultaneously being flooded by competing priorities, the solutions are going to reflect that.

As the leader, it is your responsibility to get up and out of the silos to change the organizational ecosystem. You have ultimate accountability for whatever happens in your organization, and you're also better positioned than anyone else to enable change. It's not as complicated as it might seem.

The illusions working against change are powerful, and the risk of a bad decision is not without consequence, so courage will be required.

But the performance of your organization, and the people who work there, depends on you to create this change, and it's much less scary for you to take action on organizational multitasking than for the teams you lead to do so. They have much more to lose by standing up and saying, "You know what? Something's not working here. We need to stop doing everything at the same time." Most employees are incentivized to *not speak up*.

Let's look at how this plays out in real life. Susan, a marketing director at a mid-sized agency, was confident in her ability to be a hard-driving, empathetic manager. Early on in our relationship, I asked her how she demonstrated empathy in her team. She told me a story about a time in which the agency was in the middle of merging with a former competitor. A smooth merger was the top priority for the organization, and there were many extra projects and tasks to complete. It was Susan's job to make sure it all went well.

At the same time, the agency had a record number of clients. Susan explained that her empathy showed up because at every single manager meeting, she told her direct reports to let her know if the workload was getting to be overwhelming for their teams. She said the same thing at the town hall meetings she often held with the entire department.

Susan knew the work was piling up, so she was especially proud of the fact that she made time for team-building activities at every town hall meeting. As she told me her story, it was already raising some red flags for me, like using team building to address an overwork problem (no amount of liking your coworkers is going to change the fact that you're overworked from context switching all day), but what she said next was indicative of a more troubling issue.

"Clearly, I was doing a good job," she commented, "because not a single person ever raised a hand to say the work was too much."

In my experience, the only time that most people raise their hands to say, "It's too much" is when they raise their hands to wave goodbye, which was happening a lot in Susan's organization. They endured a 43% turnover during the year of the merger. In fact, the whole reason I was there working with the group was to help them design a new team structure that would enable them to address their employee retention problem.

Susan had good intentions. She cared deeply about the people who worked for her. But she was misguided in her assumption that it was the responsibility of individuals on the team to say no to new work while they were drowning in competing priorities.

The responsibility to limit work in progress had to fall onto her, and it must fall onto you too.

To make significant cultural change and stop the flooding in your organization, you and your employees all need to be in this together—but that requires leadership. It necessitates that you, the leader, become willing to create a systemic change in the way your organization's work flows, rather than putting all your energy into managing only the symptoms of burnout after it's already taken hold.

To put it another way, you need to manage the flood, but you will always exist in a fast-paced river. And in order to navigate a fast-paced river, the way you direct the boats matters. For instance, if you let all the boats move down the river at the same time or force people to jump back and forth between boats, you're allowing a fast-paced river to turn into a potential crisis.

You need to shift the way your boats are moving down the river, and not just by getting a few rocks out of the way—that would be *reactive management*, taking place after the consequences the river has caused. You want to be proactively managing the flow of work at the start of the river. This may feel daunting, but you can do it.

LEADING IN REALITY

Ruthless Prioritization

"OVERLOADED" USED TO BE MY middle name. There are so many things that demand my attention and are worth my time. It's easy to say no to the things that don't seem worth my time. What I have found works best to manage the overload is ruthless prioritization. If I don't do it as a leader, then who will?

Ruthless prioritization demands a clear purpose. Prioritization isn't just about identifying the things that are most important or that have value.

There are so many opportunities for good, important, even essential work. So, I always need to have clarity on my intent and purpose. When a new idea emerges, I ask, "How does this fit? Is it a stronger contributor to the goal than something else that I'm doing?" If so, I'll stop doing that something else and prioritize the new idea. Stopping something that is good or useful isn't easy. That's why the prioritization must be ruthless in service of the clear purpose.

I've also come to appreciate all of the variations between no and yes. There is a spectrum: There's "No." But there is also "No, not now," "No, not yet." There are also ways to say yes without losing my focus: "Yes, I want to do this, but I can't do this right now. Could we have this meeting in three weeks and get it on the calendar?"

But if the answer is no, it's better to make that decision sooner rather than later and to communicate it. Every deferred decision comes with overhead because I'll have to revisit the decision later.

—Laura Powers, Chief Operating Officer, Business Agility Institute[42]

Raise Expectations by Solving the Right Problem

BURNOUT IS ENERGY-CONSUMING and self-perpetuating.

It fosters a monoculture: if everyone is operating on a burned-out and overworked level, no one has the brain capacity to think that perhaps things could *and should* be different. It's nearly impossible to imagine how the organizational culture might change.

In a monoculture, few can consider a divergent perspective or see things in a different way. Even when people do attempt to solve the issue, they address the wrong problem because they are too burned out to work toward the right solution.

BlackBerry, for instance, spent several years in the early 2000s trying to make more efficient keyboards. They knew that people wanted to type faster, but they were so myopically focused on the keyboard that they failed to explore the real problem: people wanted to communicate *easier*. A former colleague of mine worked at BlackBerry during this time. They shared that everyone in their division was regularly working 60+ hours a week trying to develop a better keyboard. BlackBerry experienced a huge opportunity cost pursuing the wrong technology.[43]

They solved the wrong problem and paid a huge price for it.

What's the opportunity cost your organization is facing by not addressing the underlying causes of burnout?

Start by Redefining Performance

REMEMBER HOW I PINKIE PROMISED that I would never ask you to lower your expectations? I won't. Instead, I'm going to ask you to raise your expectations. And for that, you (and everyone else) will need to stop settling for the appearance of productivity and performance rather than the real thing.

The typical understanding of performance leans toward comparison and short-term benefit. Most definitions of high performance are a variation of the dictionary definition: high performance means being "better, faster, or more efficient than others."[44]

Modern management values support this basic understanding of performance. Many of your organizations might too. However, there are two problems with defining performance in this way:

1. It favors short-term gain, with inevitable long-term costs. We've addressed some of the most harmful costs already in this chapter.

2. Defining high performance in comparison to others is inherently limiting. It perpetuates the mindset that says, "As long as we are better than our competitors, we are winning." That is a low bar for success.

I prefer author and leadership-focused researcher Marcus Buckingham's definition of high performance from his book, *The One Thing You Need to Know:* "peak performance means making the greatest possible impact over the longest period of time."[45]

In other words, performance is about maximizing human potential over the long term instead of the short term. It is about embracing the ways that real humans do great work together and amplifying the principles that lead to far-reaching, market-leading, and world-changing performance.

Burnout and high performance are fundamentally incompatible. As I will explain in the next chapter, organizational multitasking and the burnout that stems from it will always put an artificial ceiling on your performance.

Change how you define performance, and you will be freed to change the patterns that cause burnout.

CHAPTER FOUR

WHAT YOU NEED TO KNOW ABOUT ORGANIZATIONAL ECOSYSTEMS

LET'S TALK LEMONADE.

After a lesson on supply and demand, a friend of mine and some of her fellow MBA classmates had to set up a lemonade stand to study supply, demand, and market value for an assignment. The exercise was supposed to be clear-cut: manage the inputs of lemons, water, sugar, and cups; manage the output of lemonade; sell to customers; make a profit.

They tackled the assignment with creativity and the confidence of MBA grad students. While their business plan was well thought out and the math of adding up cost of supplies and subtracting that from sales revenue led them to a strong projected profit, their lemonade stand pop-up was wildly unsuccessful.

Meanwhile, my eight-year-old neighbor ends up swimming in cash whenever she sets up a lemonade stand. Why?

The real demand of a lemonade stand is an interaction with a cute kid. People who buy lemonade on the sidewalk usually aren't spending their money because they want the lemonade, but because they want to support and interact with the kids. And my neighbor isn't profitable because she's got her inputs and supply chain dialed in, she's profitable because there is a hidden infrastructure—a.k.a. parental units—supporting her entrepreneurial line of business.

While both "businesses" sold lemonade, they were, in fact, entirely different business models, built on entirely different assumptions. These different models and the beliefs, principles, and assumptions that fuel them exemplify why some organizations are more prone to the flood of organizational multitasking than others. The MBA students approached their business model like one might approach the task of understanding how a machine works: break down a lemonade business into parts so you can discover what makes a successful one, then replicate it. That led them to only see things like inputs, cost of goods, value of the lemonade, and profit. A simple, linear equation.

But performance of my neighbor's lemonade business came from a different understanding of value. Her product wasn't lemonade, it was heartwarming interactions. Her business model relied on interaction between customers, the tiny human salespeople, and the "supply chain" of adults that helped bring it together. There is nothing particularly linear about my neighbor's business.

It's a network of relationships, interactions, and, yes, ingredients. My neighbor's lemonade stand is successful because she intuitively designed it with an understanding of how people and parts interact together.

Organizational Structure

MOST ORGANIZATIONS LOOK LIKE THIS on paper:

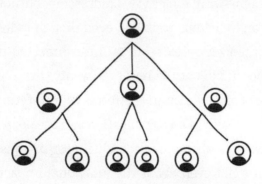

Most organizations function like this in reality:

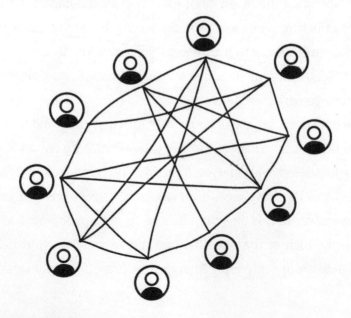

While the second drawing appears messier and more complex, it's a more accurate view of the way that a group of people interact within an organization, especially within high-performing organizations. The potential for high performance—that groundbreaking, creative, value-driven kind of performance—only exists in this interconnected reality.

Potential is unlocked in the lines between the dots.

The problem with effectively addressing burnout is that it presents as an individual problem, even though individual people within an organization exist in an interconnected network. Because collaboration is at the heart of twenty-first-century work, the outcome of our collaborative effort is what determines the performance and health of an organization and the people within it.

This book isn't about the individual cost of constant context switching. It's not even about the individual impact of burnout. It's about what happens when you have an entire organization of people spending the majority of their energy and capacity on too many competing priorities at the same time. It's about the organizational multitasking that threatens your mission, limits the value you create for your customers, and, ultimately, diminishes the outcomes you are capable of.

The question I am particularly concerned about—and that you should be concerned about too—is this: What happens in an organization when every person is persistently engaged in context switching all day long, week after week, months on end, for years?

The answer to this question, and what you can do about it, depends on which of the two drawings above matches your beliefs about how groups of people in organizations effectively work together. For you to enact the principles of flow that we will cover in the next chapter, you need to see and understand that you lead an organization more like an ecosystem and less like a machine. Even more important, you need to embrace that the seemingly messier organizational structure of an ecosystem is a good thing, not merely a reality to be tolerated.

Fundamentally, there are two competing paradigms that describe how groups of people and groups of groups of people collaborate in organizations: the *machine paradigm* and the *ecosystem paradigm.*

Some form or variation of the machine paradigm and ecosystem paradigm exists at every organization, whether you realize it or not. In fact, the beliefs, concepts, values, principles, and behaviors that make up these opposing paradigms are rarely explicit. More often, these paradigms are implicit, influencing organizational culture, structure, and decision-making without ever being named.

In this chapter, we will assess these two paradigms. It is my wholehearted belief that every leader needs a basic understanding of the differences between a machine paradigm and an ecosystem paradigm because, ultimately, you will have to choose—with intention—which model to embrace.

If you find that you want your organization to be more aligned with the machine paradigm, that's okay, but you might as well put this book down. The principles of flow and the potential for high performance cannot work in tandem with the machine paradigm—and you'll understand why by the end of this chapter.

The ecosystem paradigm, and the underlying scientific, philosophical, and social research behind it, is fascinating, but also complex and full of jargon. Systems thinking, complexity theory, Human Systems Dynamics, and chaos engineering are all related schools of thought (each with their own vocabulary of jargon) that have consumed many dissertations, global conferences, and books upon books—far more depth than I am going to explain here in this single chapter.

Instead, I endeavor to provide a straightforward explanation of each paradigm to the point that you can take the necessary actions to stop the flood of organizational multitasking and enable the flow of high performance throughout your organization.

Instead of starting with the background on where these ideas come from, adding in stories and evidence from thought leaders who make this their life's work, and then ultimately sharing my conclusion, I'm flipping it.

I'll give you my conclusion first because it may be all you need to take action. Read until you are emphatically nodding your head and underlining your favorite lines. You will then be ready to move on to the next chapter.

A machine paradigm is primarily focused on the parts of an organization:

→ the departments

→ the roles

→ the reporting structure

→ the inputs the predictable outputs that are planned[46]

In this paradigm, relationships are of secondary importance.

The Machine Pardigm

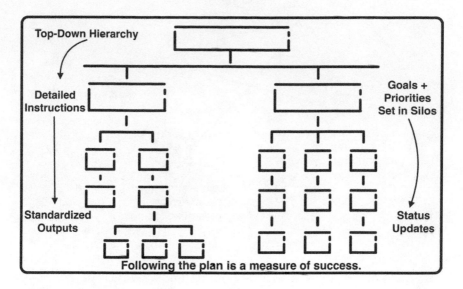

An ecosystem paradigm is primarily focused on the relationships within an organization:

→ the interactions between departments

→ the communication between people

→ the patterns of those interactions and the outcomes that emerge[47]

In this paradigm, specific parts are secondary to the value of interactions between the parts. The parts matter, but value is created through the interactions.

Ecosystem Pardigm

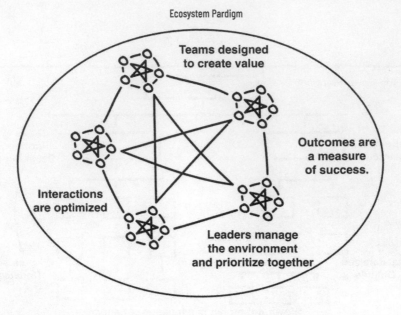

I am not at all neutral in my opinion about which paradigm is most useful for leaders. It's the ecosystem paradigm.

To stop the flood of organizational multitasking, you must embrace your role as the leader of an interconnected ecosystem and root out machine paradigm behaviors from your organization permanently.

The Definitions

Paradigm: The concepts, values, perceptions, and practices shared by a community, which form a particular version of reality that is the basis of the way the community operates.[48]

The Machine Paradigm: The belief that complex organizations can best be understood and managed like a machine with predictable parts, activities, and results.

Most organizations have at least some elements of this paradigm working in the way they organize departments, set goals, and make decisions. The problem is that these qualities usually only exist on paper, in an idealized version of themselves, not in real life. Some might point to the industrial era or to factories as an example of when the machine paradigm is appropriate, but even then, companies like Toyota have proven how limiting the mindset is.

If an organization is like a machine, it ought to be...

→ Able to be deconstructed so that its parts can be analyzed, understood, and put back together. It will operate better than ever this way.

→ Designed to only do one, *maybe* two or three, things well with predictable, repeatable precision and quality.

→ Limited to the basic math of addition and subtraction in relation to its performance. It is exactly the sum of the parts, and nothing more. It will never do anything other than what it was designed to do.

→ Able to be disassembled so parts can be removed without harming the overall function of the machine. Efficiency over effectiveness. For example, if you want a less expensive car, do you really need to have a remote start feature? Do you really need that exhaust pipe?

→ Capable of performing better by being made to work faster or cost less money. The only ways to increase performance are to reduce waste or make a part function better.

→ Completely predictable in relation to its outcomes. Its cause-and-effect relationships should be linear and clearly defined. That's how real machines ought to be, not organizations. I don't want spontaneous innovation out of my blender.

The Ecosystem Paradigm: The belief that complex organizations can best be understood and managed like a network or ecosystem. An organizational ecosystem is connected, interactive, and capable of innovation. If an organization is like an ecosystem, it is...

→ Always interacting, adapting, and evolving in order to thrive.

→ Driven by the interactions between parts.

→ Understandable only when we pay attention to the patterns that exist and the flow of information between the parts.

→ Emergent. When the parts of an ecosystem are connected, new capabilities emerge that didn't exist before and growth can become exponential.

→ Not linear when it comes to cause and effect. Change can happen in unpredictable ways.

→ Based on movement. If you want an ecosystem to perform better, pay attention to the flow of information and value throughout the organization. Find ways to remove anything that interrupts the flow.

All organizations are made up of humans working together. That is reality.

Just as our human brains exist and solve problems in particular ways (one executive function at a time—see Chapter 2), people collaborate in particular ways too. And it is easier to cultivate a healthy, high-performing ecosystem of people than it is to try to make organizations made up of people operating like machines.

Another reality is that change is everywhere, happening all the time, and unequivocally impossible to predict. We need organizations that are designed to adapt without sacrificing outcomes. If you want your organization to survive, the people who are your organization must be collaborating in ways that enable them to respond effectively to change.

It is much more effective to put your energy and resources into becoming agile and adaptive than it is attempting to predict and control change.

The Machine and Ecosystem Paradigms in Organizations

MOST ORGANIZATIONS OPERATE LIKE MACHINES, as collections of parts, because this seems like a logical way to take a big, complicated organization and make it manageable. Each area of the organization is responsible for keeping costs low and meeting revenue goals.

Get all the departments working correctly and the organization should thrive, right? Not exactly.

Cut 10% of Your Budget

"WE NEED TO CUT OVERALL operations costs by 10%," a leader might decide. "Therefore, I'll direct every department to cut 10%

of their budget." The basic math of the machine paradigm says this should work. If every department cuts 10% from their budget, the entire organization will be able to show a 10% reduction in costs. But it doesn't work that way.

The details and names in the stories that follow have been changed to protect the misguided.

Many years ago, I was hired by the CEO of a large insurance company—let's call him Tom—to guide an organizational redesign to enable more effective team collaboration. In one of our early conversations, Tom shared the painful way he came to realize that significant change was needed. The year before, Tom had told all of his direct reports that they needed to cut operation costs in their part of the organization. The chief technology officer, Tessa, had looked at their expenses and decided the best way to cut costs was to eliminate all travel.

Meanwhile, the head of Consumer Insurance Products, John, decided that the best way to cut costs would be to focus on improving the user experience on the website so the team wouldn't have to deal with as many customer service calls. However, his user experience strategy would require a more collaborative approach with the Technology group, so Patrick aimed to put together teams that would meet in person once a quarter to plan. The teams themselves, made up of people who reported to the Product leader and people who reported to the Technology leader, started getting conflicting messages about whether they would be able to travel to the in-person planning events.

The planning events started happening, but with only the team members who represented the Consumer Insurance Products team. Technology team members were not allowed to attend in person, so they had to call in over a conference line.

The result?

John got carried away with an idea, only to find out several months down the road that what they had come up with was not technologically feasible. The Technology team members on the phone hadn't been able to clearly understand what his idea was, so they had been unable to speak up or ask questions. They wasted several million dollars on planning time and delayed getting a better technology solution out to their customers by at least a year.

However, when Tom reviewed the quarterly expense reports, Tessa was congratulated; they had reduced Technology travel expenses by 50%. But overall, the company had increased operating costs because of the expensive mistakes that had occurred in the planning process.

Whether he realized it or not, Tom was operating within a machine paradigm.

He wanted to cut costs, so he had directed every executive to do so, independent of a unified strategy. The machine paradigm says that each department should be able to cut their costs because they are independent parts, or *mini machines*. Their interaction with the other departments is purely transactional.

The Technology leader cut costs, while the Consumer Insurance Products division wasn't able to. Although Tessa, the Technology leader won, the company as a whole—and even more importantly, their customers—lost.

If CEO Tom and the other leaders had been operating within an ecosystem paradigm, they would have set priorities for the company as a whole. In doing so, they may have identified customer areas in which to *invest* instead of cut. They most certainly would have started with a conversation between Tessa and John about ways to collaboratively address budget shortfalls and customer opportunities. The decisions that each leader made in isolation ignored the interactions between their departments that would have been necessary to improve customer outcomes.

Expecting each part of an organization to operate independently instead of paying attention to how the parts work together as a whole keeps you stuck in short-term thinking and creates crises. It's like cutting off one of your hands because you want to save money on gloves. If you were the glove department, you could feel proud that you cut operating expenses in half!

The Mitten Department

Snow Shoveling Department

LEADING IN REALITY

Managing Invisible Overhead

There is invisible overhead that comes from solving problems with Band-Aid solutions—because every short-term fix has to be remembered and managed. When we are only creating solutions for the surface-level symptoms that we can see, we wind up with a patchwork of Band-Aids and processes that ultimately compete with each other. And that impacts productivity, efficiency, and team morale.

Greater Twin Cities United Way is a fundraising intermediary. We partner with donors in our community to raise money for investment into our community. We are more than a pass through, we are also stewards of those investments. We must be effective and mindful in how we engage the people, systems, and workflows that contribute to getting those investments out to the universe. When the primary focus is getting dollars to the community, sometimes it's hard to see those connections.

It is important that we are communicating our value to donors, partners, and the community by practicing good stewardship through building efficient and agile systems and ways of working.

We can't afford to manage the overhead that would be created from working in silos—because what we do from an operations perspective has a significant impact on what happens in our fundraising team. It's my job as a leader to help our entire organization understand and see the connections.

—Stephannie L. Lewis, Associate Vice President of Community Impact, Greater Twin Cities United Way[49]

Monopoly Accounting

AT LARGE ORGANIZATIONS, IT'S NOT uncommon for each department to operate like their own tiny company that markets and sells to other departments. For example, the Facilities department might charge fees to the other departments for using training rooms. In other organizations, like Tom's, Technology and Product Development might be entirely separate divisions, with separate leadership, even if the products rely on technology to exist.

These tiny "companies" within companies sell their services back and forth to each other, with each department expected to show a profit at the end of each quarter. If all departments are profitable, then the company will be profitable too—or so the thinking goes. There is rarely recognition that each department is interdependent and that one department's profitability may come at the expense of another department's outcomes.

This all leads to financial gymnastics and tired people, for two reasons:

→ Real value isn't accounted for. For instance, in order for an organization to sell technology services to the Product department, the Technology division has to create some pretty complicated formulas to come up with a dollar amount to charge for the development of software. Inevitably, that dollar amount is, at best, loosely related to what it actually costs to operate the Technology teams; at worst, it's a total guess.

→ An abundance of time and energy goes into figuring out project costs. Because of the way most organizations manage human capacity—where one person is allocated X% and another allocated Y% to a project—they have to take a percentage of the employees' salaries, divide them by the percentage allocated to the project, and then make a wild guess at how long the project will take to arrive at a "cost." Coming up with these arbitrary numbers costs a lot of time and energy.

I recently saw this play out in real life when I reviewed a project plan that counted the number of people involved as actual fractions:

→   Designers: 5.34

→   Project managers: 1.28

→   Engineers: 12.87

→   Marketing coordinators: 2.12

Someone had to come up with the complicated formula to get to those numbers, and someone else got stuck with the even more intensive effort to figure out how to actually get 0.34 of a human being.

One leader I worked with called this *Monopoly accounting* because actual money wasn't being exchanged and real profit for the company never materialized. No matter how many times the Technology department sells services to the Product department, it's not until a product gets used by customers that meaningful value is created.

The Machine Paradigm Hurts Small Organizations Too

NATE SPENT THREE YEARS QUITTING his job as the program director at a mid-sized nonprofit.

The breaking point happened when Nate's first child was born. Over his time at the organization, he'd saved up about a month's worth of personal time off, which he wanted to use as paternity leave. But his boss wouldn't approve it. She told him that the organization couldn't afford to have him gone for that amount of time. He could have a week off at most.

This made sense in the short-term because she was able to keep her manager around more. But it was a massive mistake in the long term, because Nate realized that he didn't want to stay with an organization that cared so little for his family.

After he left a couple of years later, the organization experienced a 75% turnover in their core staff, the quality of their services dropped, and they ended up burning through three directors in a period of 18 months. For a small organization, the costs of hiring and replacing so many staff members in such a short time were devastating.

These are the heavy losses that can't be easily quantified or measured but are absolutely real.

Finding Flow at Toyota

A GOOD MACHINE PERFORMS THE tasks it was designed for, over and over again, with predictable quality. The machine paradigm found its beginning in the Industrial Revolution and continued to resurface in factory management throughout the twentieth century. Machines are not designed to shift and change quickly without reengineering. And so, while this idea of an "organizational machine" leads to very nice org charts and business plans, it's ineffective when it comes to responding to change or solving complex problems. It never really worked in factories, either.

In their book *The Goal*, Eliyahu M. Goldratt and Jeff Cox took a look at the Toyota Production System that transformed the company.[50] At the heart of Toyota's transformation was a shift from a machine paradigm to an ecosystem paradigm.

In the late 1940s, Toyota had a cost problem. Their margin between what it cost to make automobiles and what they brought in for revenue was shrinking. Initially, Toyota approached the problem with a machine paradigm lens, which appeared reasonable. After all, they were building automobile machines.

Their first attempt to cut costs focused on car parts. Could they use less expensive parts? Yes, they could, and they did. However, that approach quickly led to lower-quality automobiles. It wasn't going to be a long-term solution.

Intent on finding a different way to address the costs, one of Toyota's lead engineers, Taiichi Ohno, shifted his paradigm to focus on the relationship between the auto parts and the humans assembling them. Ohno paid attention to the interactions that happened during the manufacturing of the automobiles. He observed that there were huge bottlenecks in the production process that resulted in significant wasted time and money.

Instead of continuing to push for less expensive parts, Ohno focused on addressing those problems with the assembly line flow:

how the parts moved through the production process and turned into automobiles.

Toyota found that by systematically removing the bottlenecks, they were able to increase the number of automobiles produced at the factory. They increased revenue without sacrificing quality, simply by improving the flow, or interaction, between each stage of the production process.

Their approach became known as the Toyota Production System (TPS) and has been widely studied and replicated all over the world, with varying degrees of success.[51]

Toyota has been incredibly transparent about exactly what they do and how it works. In 1984, they even opened a plant in California in a joint effort with GM, a direct competitor. The NUMMI plant had many years of successful outcomes: record-breaking quality and production speed and low employee turnover.

Yet, despite having the Toyota recipe for success and even experiencing the success firsthand, GM couldn't replicate NUMMI outcomes in other plants. *This American Life* did an in-depth analysis of why TPS worked at NUMMI but failed everywhere else, ultimately ending in GM's bankruptcy in 2010.

Their conclusion?

What made TPS wildly successful in Japan and at NUMMI wasn't the new structure of the factories, the roles, or the process; it was the *trust* that existed between employees and between employees and management.[52] Managers trusted employees to speak up if and when they identified problems or had ideas for improvement, and employees trusted managers to take action. The mutual trust created a safe environment for collaborative problem-solving, even if that meant slowing down the production line.

In other words, it was the quality of collaboration that led to high-quality cars at low costs that would make any operations leader jealous.

This is ecosystem thinking at its best.

NUMMI plant leaders took care to prioritize focus, trust, and a culture of collaboration, but the rest of the GM leaders were stuck in the machine paradigm. They replicated every single component of the TPS system in at least 12 other plants. But they didn't get the Toyota outcomes because they failed to prioritize the relationships and interactions between the parts of the assembly line and the people who worked at the plant.

An Ecosystem for Healthcare

THE PROBLEM OF HIGH NURSE turnover and low patient satisfaction within the home healthcare industry in the Netherlands had been growing for years. Low patient satisfaction led to diminishing revenues. This problem was showing up on the balance sheets of many home healthcare companies.

On the surface, it seemed to be a basic math problem. Home healthcare companies needed to reduce expenses. Stuck in the machine paradigm, executives realized they could pay healthcare assistants a much lower hourly rate than they paid nurses to perform many of the services that their patients needed. If you are only looking at one part of the business model, per-patient expense, this seems like a smart business decision.[53]

But a home care health services agency is not a machine made up of parts. It's a complex network of employees, families, and healthcare providers. It's an ecosystem—whether the org chart makes that visible or not.

Jos de Blok, a home healthcare nurse, saw a different opportunity. In 2006, he founded a new company, Buurtzorg, and entered the crowded market.[54]

De Blok observed that nurses were traveling all over large metro areas to perform skilled nursing services for their rapidly growing caseloads. While many home healthcare companies were spending less on direct patient expenses, they were spending more on centralized management to coordinate nurse schedules, transportation costs, and employee turnover. As this was happening, patient satisfaction with their care and health outcomes was decreasing.

Buurtzorg did things differently. De Blok credits ecosystem thinking for the way he organized Buurtzorg. He created ecosystems called *neighborhood care teams*. Each neighborhood team was a group of highly skilled nurses responsible for the caseloads within a small geographic area. It was up to each neighborhood team to determine how to manage their schedules, patients' needs, and family communication.

The direct per-patient cost was more expensive in this model because highly skilled and highly paid nurses performed all services. However, other typical administrative costs were dramatically lower.

Buurtzorg did not need an army of coordinators and schedulers, and their transportation budget was significantly smaller than that of other similar-sized companies. More importantly, turnover among nurses was much lower than the industry averages. Patient satisfaction was high, which resulted in more referrals from physicians. Buurtzorg grew dramatically within the first few years and has continued to be an international leader in the home health-care industry.

Buurtzorg is a real example of an ecosystem paradigm at work. For de Block to be successful as an ecosystem leader, he had to be able to see the entire end-to-end experience of nurses and patients.

If de Blok were the admiral of our imaginary river filled with boats, you would find him alternating between paddling inside a boat so he could understand exactly what it was like in the middle of the raging river and up in a helicopter, observing the patterns and movements of all the people and boats down the river.

The Origins of the Paradigms

FOR THE BETTER PART OF the last century and a half, biologists, physicists, economists, management consultants, behavioral scientists, community organizers, and leaders everywhere have explored and debated these two fundamental paradigms about how humans exist together.

What these great thinkers agree on is this: the world is complex, organizations are complex, humans are complex, and we all need better ways to understand and manage this increasing complexity.

Way back in the seventeenth century, French philosopher René Descartes advocated for an "analytical" approach to understanding complexity. Take a big complex thing, Descartes essentially said, break it down into its component pieces, learn everything you can about the properties of those pieces, then put it all back together again. Do this, and you can be confident you understand everything there is to know about that big thing.[55]

Descartes's "analytical thinking" formed the basis for the machine paradigm of organizations. What he offered was logical, concrete, and easy to explain. But his paradigm was insufficient. The approach fell short as biologists and physicists continued to observe the physical world.

Observing living systems in the natural world, biologists came to understand that systems—connected groups of plants, animals, and the environment—are essential for the existence of life on our planet. In particular, it is the *interaction* between plants, animals, and the environment that sustains life.

For example, rainforests have the most diverse type of ecosystem known in the world and play a critical role in removing excess carbon from the atmosphere and slowing climate change.

While the canopy layer of trees in a rain forest does most of the heavy lifting when it comes to carbon removal, the trees by themselves aren't particularly effective. The canopy of trees only exists because of the taller, more sparse trees in the upper layer of the forest that provide just the right amount of sun to sustain the unique microorganisms on the forest floor. The microorganisms in the soil help to decompose rotting leaves, and in doing so, ensure that the soil conditions remain in perfect balance to support the towering canopy.

In contrast to biologists, physicists long believed that all physical phenomena could be reduced into smaller and smaller building blocks until eventually all that exists are subatomic particles—the building blocks of all matter.

As the field of quantum physics emerged in the 1920s, this deeply foundational belief was challenged by scientific observation.

Quantum physicists found that the smallest particles of physical matter are not particles at all. Subatomic particles are actually interconnections.

Werner Heisenberg, a pioneer in quantum physics, explained that when he observed the behavior of subatomic particles it became clear that the connections between the particles are what determined how they formed together.[56] The discoveries of quantum physicists were more similar to what biologists and biochemists were uncovering about the living world than they were to the building block theories of Descartes and Newton. Instead of focusing on parts, paying attention to relationships is the key to understanding complexity.

These ideas about complexity, relationships, and the substance of physical existence from biologists, physicists, mathematicians, chemists, and philosophers as far back as Aristotle have collectively become an interdisciplinary field of study called *systems thinking.*

The field of systems thinking that emerged in the twentieth century provided a stark contrast to the predominant beliefs in the emerging world of organizational management. In the 1950s, while Ohno of Toyota was applying systems thinking to what would become known as the Toyota Production System, the organizational principles of scientific management, first popularized by Frederick Taylor in the early twentieth century,[57] were gaining steam.

Because this is just a single chapter and not a dissertation, I will refrain from expounding on all the ways scientific management was wrong. I encourage you to read Edward Deming's book *The New Economics* for a detailed critique.[58] What you need to know is that scientific management, or Taylorism, as the method came to be known, was not at all grounded in the actual scientific observations of complex organizations. Scientific management was wholly based on the machine paradigm, focusing on efficiency in each part of the organization to return maximum short-term profits.

Okay, so what does all of this have to do with organizational multitasking, burnout, and high performance?

Jump back over to the raging river filled with boats that represent your most important initiatives, goals, and projects. The machine paradigm leads to the erroneous belief that people and projects can be divided into parts. In theory, one person can captain five boats, as long as they spend 20% of their time in each boat. But you know by now how much it costs to jump back and forth across those boats.

Machine thinking incubates those illusions about performance, whereas the ecosystem paradigm helps us see the ways that seemingly unrelated problems are actually connected, like the relationship between organizational multitasking and burnout. A boat captain who is managing five boats simultaneously doesn't spend much time actually leading, and the ecosystem paradigm helps us understand why that's so problematic.

Systems thinking as a school of thought exists to help us all understand the complexity of how people work together, why change happens, and how to move forward in real life. It's not easy. Yet I maintain that understanding how to manage in the ecosystem paradigm is essential for every effective leader.

What Is Possible in an Ecosystem Paradigm

AN ORGANIZATIONAL ECOSYSTEM CAN TAKE on three basic patterns:

1. **It can be organized and healthy: the whole of the ecosystem is greater than the sum of its parts.** Here's what that means. You can have a lump of graphite (the whole) that is made of carbon atoms (the parts). However, when the conditions of heat and pressure are just right, that lump of graphite turns into a diamond (the greater whole).

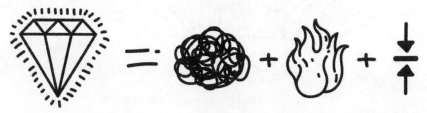

The whole (the diamond) is greater than the sum of its parts (graphite + heat + pressure).

2. **It can be disorganized and weak: the whole of the ecosystem is less than the sum of its parts.** This is exactly what is happening in the Great Barrier Reef off the coast of Queensland, Australia. Coral reef ecosystems are made up of more than 7,000 species of living organisms, and for thousands of years, the Great Barrier Reef has effectively purified water, removed carbon from the atmosphere, and helped to regulate ocean temperatures. However, climate change and toxins in the ocean have damaged the reef, causing the interdependent relationships between organisms in the reef to weaken (e.g., the algae that cover the cor-

al and protect it from sunlight are dying, so the coral itself is becoming less efficient at purifying water).[59] What was once a thriving and healthy ecosystem is becoming disorganized, weak, and at risk of disappearing entirely. This is also what happens in a state of unending context switching. It's why, as we know from Chapter 2, you cannot divide your capacity into parts and expect that it will all add back up to 100%.

Coral Reefs are becoming unhealthy ecocsystems.

3. **It can be neutral: the whole is exactly the sum of its parts and will never be anything more.** Imagine a key and a lock (the two parts). The purpose of the key is to enable limited access to a room (the whole). However, the key cannot per-form its function without the lock. In fact, the lock must be designed with the specific key in mind. The lock and key form a system, but they will likely never perform beyond their original intent. This is the uninspiring scenario that can happen if you work to develop an efficient organization that lacks vision and outcomes. It will produce some results, but it will never be capable of true innovation.

A lock + key will do their job but will never innovate on their own.

You want the first kind of ecosystem. An organized and healthy organizational ecosystem includes the possibility of evolution and emergence, the possibility that a new idea could emerge that never existed before. This kind of ecosystem delivers high performance, the kind that is capable of innovation with no limit to what is possible, and it is also the path forward to solving the problem that made you pick up this book: the flood of organizational multitasking.

LEADING IN REALITY

Expanding Capacity

SOME OF MY BEST INSIGHTS and ideas come when I am engaged with people outside of my direct department or division. Recently, I participated in a roundtable discussion with leaders from across Mayo Clinic. After that conversation, I noticed that I was energized beyond what I had been feeling lately. There was a particular problem on my mind, and a comment that someone made caused me to think about the problem from an entirely different vantage point. When I did so, the possible solutions I could envision changed.

So often, when we talk about managing our capacity, we think it means that we either have to decrease the amount of work we do or add more people to our team. But that's a limiting way to think about capacity. We can also expand our creativity and capacity by finding unexpected connections and divergent perspectives.

—Jen Roelke, Senior Director, Digital Talent Strategy, Mayo Clinic[60]

The views expressed are the author's personal views, and do not necessarily reflect the policy or position of Mayo Clinic.

Why Your Ecosystem Matters

YOU CAN STOP THE FLOODING. You can be an ecosystem leader.

But you can't do it alone.

The illusions and lies that keep your organization in a constant state of flooding are powerful. Because of the shared cultural experiences and years of working in a flood that result from the machine paradigm, fully embracing the ecosystem paradigm for your organization will demand a significant mindset shift around how you lead and how everyone gets work done.

You can read about why this shift matters so much, you can hear stories about how others have done it, you can want to make the shift too. But when you put this book down, the illusions and promises of modern management are going to be whispering in your ear that this isn't the path for you.

Shifting your mindset around success and performance is simple, but it's not easy. It's not easy because the same part of your brain that is responsible for shifting a mindset is the same part of your brain responsible for goal shifting and rule activation.

Once you set this book down, all the competing priorities and tasks at hand will come flooding back. Your brain can only perform one executive function task at a time, so mindset shifting won't be at the front of the queue.

This pattern of wanting to make change but getting caught in a cycle of too much to do is like a whirlpool where water just swirls in circles, pulling you into a downward spiral—you can't survive the mindset shifting whirlpool alone. If you try to act on your own, without creating space for others to unpack these same problems, you won't succeed.

The forces are too great around you. But you don't have to fail.

The good news is that you aren't starting from zero. Ecosystems are already a reality in your organization. You don't need to create one in your organization because it's already emerging whether you want it to or not. Right now, you might have an ecosystem that is not thriving. Without effective leadership, your ecosystem will be disorganized and weak, like the Great Barrier Reef. Without clear vision your ecosystem might be neutral, like a key and lock—everything works, but it's not innovative. You have the opportunity to shape your ecosystem into a high-performing one, capable of emerging levels of performance that are greater than the sum of their parts, just like a rain forest or a diamond. I want that high-performing ecosystem for your organization. It's absolutely possible, and in the next chapter, I'll show you how to make it happen.

For now, the most impactful way to get out of the whirlpool and into action is to bring your peers and teams into the conversation.

Start by exploring the machine and ecosystem paradigms. Where do each of them show up in your organization? When and where do you emphasize the parts of your organization, and when do you pay attention to relationships?

The rest of the book is focused on specific steps you, as an ecosystem leader in your organization, can take to end the flood of organizational multitasking. What follows is not all you will need to solve every problem in your organizational ecosystem, but it will make every single problem you encounter easier to solve.

CHAPTER FIVE

GET FLOW AND END THE FLOOD

IT'S TIME TO TALK ABOUT FLOW.

First, let's start by defining it.

I've said a few times that flow is the opposite of flood, but what does that really mean?

In more concrete terms, flow is how work gets done with ease. Flow happens when a project, a goal, an initiative, a task, etc. moves through idea to execution unimpeded. Ideas create value only when they get used, so improving the way work flows through your organization is the most effective way to improve the value you deliver. And the more value that actually flows, the more value you deliver.

Flow is what happens when important work is accomplished with momentum and excellence, with people who are deeply engaged and working at a sustainable pace, resulting in increased productivity and higher performance.

Flow is the experience of energy, creativity, and value moving from ideas to results throughout your entire organization. When your organization has flow, collaboration feels powerful, and people are more excited about the outcomes than about taking credit for their individual contributions.

Flow is the reason a complex project goes better than expected and creative ideas emerge from unexpected places. It is what happens when the final outcome is greater than anything that any one person could have done on their own. The work may not be easy, but there is a feeling of ease, clarity, and purpose.

Flow is the opposite of flood.

You can shape the change required to enable powerful flow of value through your entire organization. You can do this even if you are flooded by competing priorities right now.

I know it's possible because I've seen it and have guided it over and over again, from global companies that lead the S&P 500 to neighborhood-based organizations that lead their community gardens.

The following is a guide to help you find real flow too.

1. Visualize Everything

THE VERY FIRST STEP IS to make your work more visible. Physically visible.

This isn't a meditative exercise where you manifest the world you want by drawing a picture. It's a practical exercise in transparency, where making the work of your organization physically easier to see is the first step in leading your ecosystem.

Why? Because you can't lead what you can't see.

Visualizing work enables you to see the flow: how work (and, more importantly, value) moves through your organization at the top level, all the way down to individual teams, and how work moves through teams to get done and deliver value.

Most people have a limited understanding of how their daily work contributes to organizational goals and objectives. One study of over 5,000 employees across dozens of companies found that less than one-third of team members could name how their daily work contributed to the strategic objectives of their companies.[61] Even fewer people are likely to understand what other teams in the organization are doing, how that work connects to their work, and how it all fits together to solve problems.

I once worked with an organization that had four departments paying five different consultants to help them do customer insights work. Because of the way this company organized their departments, they were all working on different products, but ultimately, it was the same customer group that they were serving.

How did they discover this overlap? When I was facilitating a strategic planning retreat, leaders put their initiatives up on the wall. Prior to this exercise, they had had approximately zero understanding of the objectives the other departments were pursuing.

Don't judge them too harshly. It's a common problem. In a survey of over 100 companies, representing two million employees, more than half of the respondents reported not even knowing what their company's top goals were for the year.[62]

In an era of more remote work than ever before, this problem intensifies. The program director at a large science museum recently told me, "Everyone knows what our top goal is right now." When I surveyed her team of 10 people, though, I got 8 unique responses to the question, "What's your organization's top priority?"

Only one of the answers was the same as the director's.

Instead of embracing an organizational ecosystem, we tend to silo everybody into separate departments with separate objectives. The result is that even you as a leader wind up in the middle of a raging, fast-moving river, without clarity on the shared outcomes. You're jumping back and forth between boats all day, trying to move them forward and deal with the urgent problems that come up along the way.

When you spend your time in that way, it's almost impossible to get that bird's-eye view to see the entire river. As a result, you can't see the whole system: what's happening upstream, what's happening downstream, what work is getting done, and where there are bottlenecks.

Imagine that you're at a river and one of your boats starts to crash into a rock. You're going to go to that boat and you're going to help them figure things out, but you're not going to be very aware of what's happening in the other boats. You won't be paying attention to anything upstream, and it will be hard to look around at what is downriver.

You can't see the entire flow of the river if you are in a boat. You can't even see the whole river from the dock. You have to get up into the air.

How to Make Your Work Visible

There is a Japanese word, *kanban*, which roughly translates to "visual signal" or, in some circumstances, *the work you can see*.[63] It's become the term to describe an organizational discipline that emerged through the practices of Toyota and lean manufacturing to provide guidance on how to see and improve workflow.

Kanban is a framework that encourages leadership at all levels of an organization to learn and improve together. The most basic principle of Kanban is to make work visible. This is often done with a *Kanban board*. In this book, I'm teaching an adapted approach to Kanban. For that reason, I prefer to call it a *flow board*, because flow of work is exactly what we are aiming to see more clearly.

It's easy to create a simple flow board. Here's how to get started.

1. **Identify all the boats in your river**—all of the projects, all of the initiatives, all of the products, all of the objectives and goals, the things that you are trying to accomplish in your organization—and put them up on a wall. My favorite way to do this is on an actual physical wall, but virtual walls can work too. Put only one thing on each sticky note, and place every sticky note up on the wall.

!! Tip: *Pick your scale. Are you mapping out enterprise initiatives? Line of business objectives? Team-level goals? Your personal priorities for the week? You can do this exercise at any scale, but it helps to identify a target level of detail before you start.*

Create a Flow Board

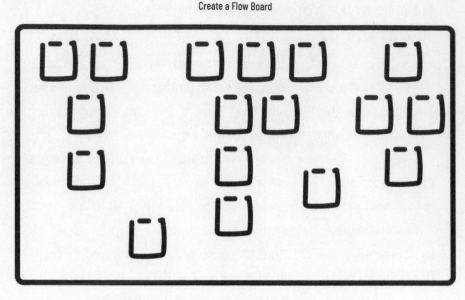

Step 1: Put all of your boats (initiatives,projects, goals) on a wall of sticky notes.

2. **Organize it.** Group your sticky notes into one of three categories. These categories are the foundation of a flow board.

TO DO: Everything that is on your radar but that no one is working on yet. Perhaps this includes the revamp of the performance evaluations that needs to get done or preparing for the quarterly board meeting or the market-research project that is slated to start next week.

DOING: Everything that is in your portfolio *and* in progress. People are actively working on these items but aren't finished yet.

DONE: As in, *done*. Finished. Shipped. People can now use what was created and are (hopefully) getting value from it.

Create a Flow Board

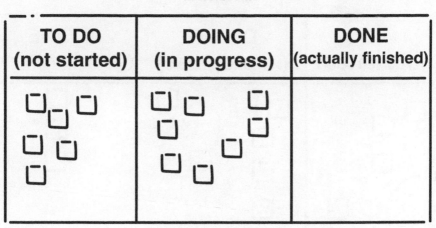

TO DO (not started)	DOING (in progress)	DONE (actually finished)

Step 2: Organize the sticky notes

3. **Observe the board.** Spend a week updating the board, moving items that are completed to **done** and adding anything that is started to the **doing** column. How big is your **doing** category growing? How many new priorities get added to the **to-do** column?

This is how you start to see the flow and the flood in your organization. How often does work move from **doing** to **done**? Or does everything just get backed up, in a perpetual state of **doing** without any visible progress being made? Do your columns swell with more **to dos** and more **doings**, adding to the flooding tax you're paying by doing too many things at the same time?

Create a Flow Board

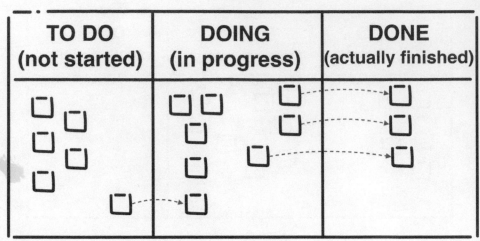

Step 3: Observe + track the flow.

This is the data leaders need in order to understand the way work flows in their ecosystem. Within this data are critical clues that will make some of your most perplexing, difficult problems— the ones that keep everyone in a state of overwhelming, underperforming flood—recognizable.

There are many different ways to construct a flow board like this. The only requirement I'll give you is that it has to be visible and accessible to everyone for organizational transparency. If the board is hidden away, the flow (or flood) of work won't be as easily tracked, the board won't get updated as much, and work ultimately won't be visible.

Ugly and useful is better than pretty and hidden. Don't create this board in a fancy tool (The Fancy Boat Illusion could trap you here too) that no one else will have access to and that you will never open. That is not visible, nor is it transparent and accessible.

One chief executive officer I worked with did this exercise with the company's operating committee. She asked her office manager to figure out a way to move their wall of sticky notes from the retreat into the executive boardroom. The brilliant office manager re-created the board and placed it on a rolling whiteboard directly outside of the CEO's office. The CEO had to walk by it every time she entered or left her office.

This CEO told me that the simple act of seeing the work multiple times a day changed her focus in a profound way.

Two Main Reasons Your Work Doesn't Flow

As you start to visualize your work through the lens of a flow board, you may find things aren't flowing as much as you'd like them to. Below are two of the most common reasons why.

1. It's hard to know when an effort should be moved from **doing** to **done**.

You may find that it's hard to identify the difference between **doing** and **done** because your goal is not very well defined. Vague goals suck time, energy, and money from every single person who tries to achieve them. If the desired outcome is ambiguous, then no one knows what the real expectation is.

For example, "grow our client base" is effectively a useless goal when it comes to knowing the difference between **doing** and **done**. Something like "increase new client engagements by 10%" would be much more helpful because it's specific and quantifiable.

A good target should pass The Champagne Test: *How will we know when we've accomplished this objective and can pop a bottle of champagne to celebrate?*

If the target is not precise, then you don't have clarity on when you will be able to get value from that effort. And if you don't have clarity on this, then no one else will either.

Lack of clarity introduces huge risks. It's also a reason why so many organizations expend time and energy feeling busy but don't get observable results.

Pay attention to when an effort moves from **doing** to **done**. Doing so will reveal where you have alignment, clarity, and flow, or it will expose where ambiguity is sabotaging your flow and contributing to the flood.

2. Your boats are too big.

The other reason you might be having a hard time seeing flow is because your boats are too big. A barge moves slowly down a river and gets blocked easily. Similarly, you might not be seeing movement over the course of a week or a month because your chunks of work are too big. Big efforts of work that aren't broken down into smaller slices of value move slowly and quickly cause bottlenecks.

A healthcare system I worked with had a large strategic initiative to expand their service area into neighboring towns. That was almost verbatim the objective when I first started working with them: "expand into two new communities."

Achieving that objective might take two to three years. That "barge" of a project could sit in progress forever; you would never see it move. However, there are a lot of steps along the way that are going to need to happen to get to that end goal. And there may be an opportunity to take that huge initiative and break it down into some more concrete strategic objectives and key results that can be carved out to produce value and start providing a return on investment sooner.

The strategy team responsible for expanding the healthcare system into those new communities developed an "outcomes roadmap" instead of a project plan. The work ahead of them was going to be complex, and while they could identify some of the key activities and milestones along the way, this team, using their ecosystem lens, knew that there was no linear path to their big goal. The outcomes roadmap included smaller—yet valuable— outcomes. Since they were in the early stages of this strategic initiative, they focused on defining short- to mid-range outcomes. Some of those outcomes included forming community advisory teams, completing public health needs assessments, and designing community-informed development plans.

The strategy team took time to create measurable success criteria and a "definition of done" for each outcome. From there, other teams could take responsibility for the actual execution of each outcome. And all the while, progress was visible and transparent along the way.

Tips and Traps When Making Your Work Visible

The Start Where You Are Right Now Tip

WHEN YOU FIRST START OUT, begin with just one area of your organization. It will be tempting to include everything in your entire organization on the wall, but this is a time to put a boundary around just one particular area of the organization that you influence. Don't take on the whole just yet.

When you are in the middle of the flood, if you don't already have a clear view of your whole ecosystem, it can be overwhelming to get everything up on the wall. Start with what you can see from where you are.

The Zoom Out or Zoom In Tip

IF YOU ARE GETTING STUCK on what to put on your sticky notes, change your scale. It may be helpful to zoom out and start at a 30,000-foot view: strategic priorities, goals, objectives, and initiatives. Put them on sticky notes and indicate what's in progress, what's coming up, and what's done.

Alternatively, zoom way in. Focus on just your personal work or the work of just one team.

At first, it doesn't matter what scale you use; it just matters that everything on your board has a similar scale. As you get more practice, you can add layers and integrate different scales within your organization. But for now, pick your boundary, pick the team or the area that you're going to focus on, and put everything up on the wall.

The Tool Trap

YOU MIGHT BE TEMPTED TO do all of this on a spreadsheet because those boxes are super easy to organize. You can fit a lot of information into a small area on a spreadsheet. But resist that temptation.

The goal is to make everything *easier* to see. Spreadsheets, on the other hand, make everything smaller and more complicated, especially when you are getting started.

Equally tempting, you may want to investigate the most robust enterprise workflow tools available for purchase, the ones with all the shiny features. Don't.

These strategies keep your work locked in a tiny screen away from people, and that is a problem. It's one of the challenges that comes with virtual collaboration. When all of our work happens on small screens, we lose the visual benefit of literal big walls.

However, there are a few ways to overcome this challenge, even if you are in a remote work environment:

→ Use wall space in your work area, even if your colleagues don't share it. Using your own personal wall or giant sticky notes will help you synthesize your own thinking first.

→ Invest in real-time collaboration tools that allow multiple people to work in the same virtual document simultaneously. A real-time virtual whiteboard that allows everyone to contribute will be much more effective than a spreadsheet or specialized tool.

→ Eventually, you will probably need a software tool that can help everyone in your organization see and manage the flow of work from idea to **done**. When you evaluate these tools, look for options that make information more transparent and more accessible instead of harder to access.

Searching out the perfect tool first is an avoidance tactic; it's the complexity bias at work. It will keep you from reckoning with reality. Don't get sucked into the tool trap.

The Make It Bigger Tip

WHETHER IT'S DONE IN PERSON or spread across time zones, the work of your organization is still plentiful and complex—the most important work always is. One of the strategies for making meaning out of those details and making decisions in those spaces is to literally make documentation of the work bigger. Give it more space on the page.

Your brain is more easily able to process information when you go from trying to make meaning of 100 different projects on a spreadsheet to 100 different projects on a big wall.[64] When you make the information larger, it becomes simpler to see and easier for your brain to process.

The Delegating Trap

YOU MIGHT GET STARTED AND decide that getting your work into a flow board is something you should delegate. Stop right there.

This is your work to do as the leader of your ecosystem. You may not have all the information—and you should definitely invite others to work through the process with you—but do not delegate the work of putting everything up on the wall. At least, not when you are just getting started.

If the inspiration to change doesn't come from you, everyone else is going to have a much harder time making a change. Remember how hard it is for an employee to speak up to their higher-ups, risk their job, and say, "I'm drowning. We need to do something about this." That's probably not going to happen. Team members need to hear and see their leaders do the work of changing.

This is your work to do, and no one else's.

The Benefits of Making Your Work Visible

THERE ARE TWO REASONS WHY making your work visible will make your job easier. The first is *being able to see the future.*

When you can see the flow of work in your organization, you can see exactly what's going on at any given time. You will be able to "see the future" because you know what's coming upstream and downstream. The more you observe the flow of work, the more you'll be able to see the patterns that repeat themselves over and over again in your organization. When you recognize the pattern, you can anticipate what's coming next. Sure, you won't be able to literally predict the future, but at least you'll be able to see some of it coming.

The second reason is that you'll experience *instant, radical transparency.*

When you make the priorities, initiatives, efforts, goals, opportunities, and work visible, you no longer have to hold it all in your head or worry that you (or someone else) are missing something. This practice takes the huge burden off your brain, your physical body, and everyone around you.

In seeing the flow of work and making it visible, you immediately create transparency—transparency for yourself, but also for your co-leaders, peers, and everybody who is part of your organization.

LEADING IN REALITY

The Work You Can See (And the Work You Can't See)

I FIND IT INCREDIBLY VALUABLE for teams to take a bird's-eye view of their work from time to time. I have teams create a big chart of different categories of work in their backlog, how often they typically received this type of request in a month, where the request typically comes from, and whether they feel they can service the monthly volume without working overtime.

Recently I asked a team to do this exercise because some leaders in the organization were wondering why the team had a hard time completing their planned work. The activity revealed that only a portion of their work was being tracked. All of the support request tickets and customer service chat interactions were left out of the official data. By having the team themselves create a chart that showed the flow of their work, we got ballpark data in a short period of time.

When this team shared their visual chart with their leader, she was so excited to see this holistic picture of the team's demand that she brought her other team leads over to show them and asked that each of them do the same thing.

The team leads were surprised to see the high volume of work represented holistically. They had been feeling that the volume of work and the overtime hours were adding up, but until they took the time to document it as a whole team, they didn't really understand the drivers of the overwork.

I helped to aggregate and package this information across the teams and joined the team leaders in presenting the results—the percentage of teams who were struggling to service the demand and the actions the teams and team leads were taking to address the challenge. (We presented this without the team names attached to the charts because the goal was to show this as an organizational challenge, not as a way to compare teams.)

Over the course of a few months of working with this transparent view, we started to notice changes in behavior. The leaders under the department head were more active in the planning events, meeting with each team during the day to ensure they were not overloading themselves and helping with real-time prioritization decisions, as well as providing this air coverage after planning. The teams were working their action plans and getting support from leaders. Within a year, teams improved their predictability by almost 40% and felt more comfortable discussing prioritization and trade-offs.

—Marie Dingess, Agile Portfolio Lead, Capital One[65]

This level of transparency may initially feel uncomfortable because everyone will see the bottlenecks, the multitasking, and the impediments that slow everyone down. Take heart; it won't always feel that way. Push past the discomfort. When everyone can see the problems, everyone can also help solve them.

When you start to enact the flow principles, you will reveal what your real problems are. One of the heavy losses that happens in a flooding organization is that you wind up solving the wrong problems or you only ever see the symptoms of the problems. So, unless you can get to the real issues, you will always underperform.

This is why, if you are only going to do one thing to enable flow and stop the flood, making your work visible is the most essential step.

2. Limit Your Work In Progress

"WORK IN PROGRESS" IS ANYTHING that has been started but is not done. In other words, it's not creating any value (yet). If something in progress suddenly cannot be finished or is no longer needed, then the work already completed is waste. Thus, "work in progress" represents liability and cost, while work "done" represents value. Work in progress is everything in your **doing** column on the flow board.

A *work in progress limit* (WIP limit) is a boundary around the amount of work that you are doing at any given time. In the most straightforward way, it means that you voluntarily limit the number of efforts in progress and will not start a new one until you finish one.

Recall our experiment in Chapter 2, where we juggled cups of water across the room. At one point, you had four "cups in progress," all in some stage of transport, all at risk of spilling and slowing you down. If you were to set a work in progress limit for juggling water, for most people, it would be two cups of water in transport at any given time. You have two hands; you can hold a cup of water in each hand easily without spilling. Two is a natural limit for carrying cups of water.

But this doesn't mean that you'll only move two cups across the room. It means that you'll prioritize which two cups to carry first, get those to their destination, and then come back for two more.

Even though that might seem inefficient, it's much faster and more effective than attempting to exceed your limit by carrying all the cups at the same time, stressed and spilling along the way. Not only that, but you'll avoid dropping the occasional third cup. And, even better, the water in those first two cups can be used, adding value, even while the other cups are transported, creating a more continuous flow of water across the room.

If we are looking at the river filled with boat captains jumping in and out of their moving boats, I might determine, after seeing that a boat captain can safely guide one boat down the river at a time, that one boat is the work in progress limit for a boat captain. When a captain starts to jump from boat to boat and has to direct multiple boat crews, safety and quality start to suffer.

Captains and crew should have a WIP limit of one boat at a time because guiding a boat down a fast-moving river is challenging and requires constant attention. If the effort is less demanding, you may be able to manage a higher WIP limit, but there is always a limit beyond which quality and effectiveness start to suffer.

WIP limits are not just an individual reality; they also exist at the group or ecosystem level. Your job is to discern how many boats your entire river can handle at a time. What is your group's collective work in progress limit?

If you are the admiral of this fleet of boats in the river, you should pay attention to how many boats can be moving down the river simultaneously. You don't want jams, but you also don't want to have idle time.

That means you need to figure out how many boats can be in the water, while paying attention to quality, outcomes, and human constraints. If you have 12 boat captains, then 12 is probably your "boat in progress" limit. However, you may have 12 boat captains but notice that every time there are more than seven boats in the water, the number of accidents increases. Perhaps seven would be the limit that you need to honor in that case.

But you aren't actually the admiral of a fleet of river boats. So, here's how that concept plays out in the real world of work.

A small financial services technology company came to me because they were struggling with high turnover and a shrinking user base, and their math wasn't adding up. They were investing significantly in talent development, but a recent engagement survey revealed that employees were overworked, averaging a 65-hour workweek.

Employees were putting in so much effort with few of the desired results.

When we got all their work up on the board, the problem became visible. They had 10 teams. Each team had 10 projects in their backlog, all in some stage of progress. That's 100 projects in progress across the organization, all of which were "critical."

Even though they were all "critical," none of the projects got more than a fraction of attention because everyone was context switching so much and so fast that they literally didn't have the brainpower to create any kind of real progress.

The CEO, Marta, knew that prioritization mattered. The previous year, an expensive consultant had led the organization through a prioritization exercise in which everyone got $100 of Monopoly money to "spend" on the projects and new features they believed were most important.

While the intentions were good, the practice was misguided. The outcome was a long list of important priorities that people were willing to spend money on, rather than effective prioritization.

Everyone at the company knew what the priorities were, and everyone was phenomenally busy working on them. But collectively, they had no idea what was keeping them so busy, and they weren't seeing the results of all that effort. They were barely treading water.

Boundaries exist, whether or not we acknowledge them. A WIP limit is a version of a boundary. This company had so far exceeded the natural boundaries of what their ecosystem could handle that they were losing customers and employees and watching their vision for the future disintegrate.

They could have chosen a complicated set of initiatives to improve morale. They could have invested more into their marketing campaign. They could have preached about the importance of quality and sent everyone to a workshop on how to be better software engineers. These have the appearance of being reasonable solutions if you are only looking at one problem at a time through a machine paradigm lens.

But once these leaders made their flow of work more visible, a different perspective emerged. They began to see the reality that every single team was flooded with competing priorities, trying to make progress on everything at the same time, and that was the reason very little was getting done.

If there is anything close to organizational magic, it is the discipline of limiting work in progress. It is both a natural boundary and a skill. You can develop both.

A work in progress limit is not magic because it will solve your problems. A work in progress limit is magic because it will make every problem easier to solve.

How to Find Your Work in Progress Limit

Figuring out what the right work in progress limit is for your organization is more of an experiment than a formula.

A limit that is too small will result in idle teams and minimal flow of value. A limit that is too large will cause organizational flooding. The only promise I can make to you is that you will change your work in progress limit as you experiment to find how many boats of work your organization can effectively flow down your river.

Start experimenting with WIP limits in an area where you are fully empowered to set boundaries and are accountable for the outcomes. That might mean you start with a single team, or you might be positioned to identify a work in progress limit for your entire company.

Once you identify your organizational area, use these questions to explore what a good WIP limit might be:

1. What is your area of accountability? Define the beginning and end of the ecosystem that you are managing.

2. How many "boats" do you have in progress right now?

3. How many teams or groups of people working together are dedicated to this work? (This will be the number to start with as your first work in progress limit.)

WIP limits are not universal; they are particular to the nature of your work and the unique people who are doing the work. The only universal truth is that WIP limits will change over time as you start to see both your work and people more clearly. Finding the right WIP limit depends on a variety of factors, and the best way to figure it out is to experiment.

Limit Work in Progress (WIP)

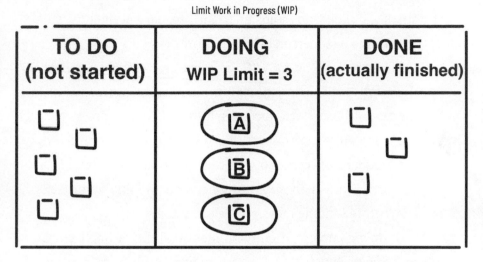

As leader of the company, Marta ultimately had accountability for the health of the entire ecosystem. The company decided to implement an organizational WIP limit of 10. They had 10 teams, so a work in progress limit of 10 was a fine starting point.

The organization agreed that for the next six months they would hold a limit of 10 projects, goals, efforts, features, opportunities, etc. Given that they wanted to go from over 100 "boats" in progress at the same time to just 10, the CEO asked for an explicit commitment from each senior leader to honor the overall work in progress limit.

But their story doesn't end there.

How to Honor a Work in Progress Limit

Have you ever been to one of those gigantic waterslides where you first spend 25 minutes climbing up six stories, only to whoosh down the slide in approximately 93 seconds? Have you ever noticed that, in order to keep everyone safe, they have a *one person on the slide* limit? Perhaps you've noticed a lifeguard down at the bottom of the slide who radios up to the lifeguard at the top when it's safe for the next person in line to come down.

This is essentially how a WIP limit operates. It creates a feedback loop between starting, finishing, and starting again.

This feedback loop introduces a self-managing quality mechanism. In our waterslide example, if a kid at the bottom of the slide lets the lifeguard know that one of the screws is loose around the second turn, there is an opportunity to halt the line and fix the problem before sending more people down the slide.

At Marta's company, each team identified the effort that was closest to being finished and agreed to work on only that project until it was *done*—because once it was done it could be used, thus adding value. The leadership team agreed to support the teams' decisions. The entire company used a high-level flow board to track the work.

When teams are working at their max work in progress limit, leaders have the job of managing the emerging priorities and solving problems that are getting in the way of teams finishing work.

This is exactly what the company's leaders did. Progress was being made, teams felt focused, and employees got a lot done because they didn't have to context switch as much as they had been. Everyone was happy and worked peacefully. The end.

For about three days.

This was March 2020. In the midst of their internal efforts to end the flood of competing priorities and multitasking, a global pandemic was unfolding. The United States Congress authorized a small-business payroll protection loan program that relied on existing banks for implementation.

The needs of the company's small-business customers shifted dramatically. The company needed to design a digital loan application process that complied with the new mandate, and they had about a week to do it.

If a new, super-critical, extra-important priority emerges, you have two options, maybe three. In the old way of doing things, you'd look at your teams and figure out where you could theoretically squeeze out a little more "capacity" so that this new, super-important thing could get started.

But the leaders of this company had agreed to honor the WIP limit. "Just get started" was not one of their options.

When you have a very human, very real work in progress boundary in place, *and* you need to get started on something new, you must decide which current work in progress should go on hold to make room for the new priority.

That is option one: **a trade-off**.

Option two is to **wait to start until something else gets done**.

Option three is to **hire more people**.

If you choose option one, the new, super-important thing goes to the very top of your "do-next" list. You choose what to bump from the **doing** list to the backlog. The minute the work in progress of your teams drops below 10, they can get started on the next highest priority. In the meantime, you can focus on removing any impediment that risks slowing your teams down so that they are able to effectively get to **done** on their current work.

If option two, waiting to start, doesn't seem palatable, then your third option is to hire more people to form another team and increase the capacity of your ecosystem. In my experience, when the "just get started" option that used to be the go-to is no longer available, "hire more people" is usually the favorite choice of leaders new to work in progress limits. It's the machine paradigm at work, whispering in the ears of stressed leaders that more "parts" would make things move faster. However, "hire more people" rarely works to solve problems that are urgent and have competing priorities. See Chapter 3 for a refresher on the time and expense of onboarding new team members.

The "hire more people" solution is as useful in a crisis as it would be for the water park manager to suggest that they should just build another slide as soon as possible to reduce a long line. It takes too long to solve the immediate problem.

"Wait" and "hire another team" were not viable options for Marta's company. Instead, they made a trade-off decision—in this case, a big trade-off. Because speed was essential, they put four of their top 10 priorities on hold, reducing their work in progress limit to six items instead of 10. Now four teams had open capacity to take on the highest-priority work: figuring out how to get the small-business loans to go live at the end of the week.

It initially might feel counterintuitive to limit work in progress for ourselves or our teams because the practice runs counter to our deeply ingrained belief about high performance that more is always more.

But wait.

This isn't as foreign of an idea as it may seem to be at first glance. We limit our work in progress all the time.

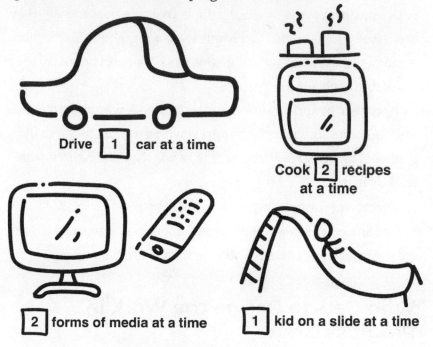

Humans limit work in progress everywhere but work.

How many cars can you drive? How many meals can you cook at the same time? If you are the parent of young children, you might have some skills in cooking two meals simultaneously, but you probably wouldn't take on four different dinner menus in a single cooking session. You might flip back and forth between a movie and reading the news on your tablet, but you probably won't attempt to watch three movies at the same time.

All around us, every single day, we use WIP limits. They only feel counterintuitive in the world of modern management, where we consistently try to bend reality to get more started.

WIP limits result in more getting done and, therefore, higher performance across the entire organization.

Marta's company met their goal of launching the new small-business loans by the deadline. Over the next month, they processed $30 million in forgivable loans for their small-business customers and picked up new customers because of how easy they made it to apply for the loan.

By the end of April, their surprise top priority was accomplished. They now had six "boats" in progress with a work in progress limit of 10. The question then became, *What should these four teams work on next?*

That is a performance question.

The answer lies in whatever effort, upon completing it, will create the most value or address the next most critical problem.

Who Gets to Define the Work in Progress Limit?

This brings us to our final question regarding WIP limits.

The answer is simple: *the people doing the work get to define the WIP limit.*

You can only define and control your own work in progress limit and cannot tell any other group what their internal work in progress limit should be. You can only require that they have a work in progress limit and use it to increase their flow of value.

In the middle of a conversation on exactly this question, the leader of a marketing agency got quiet and said, "But if the teams can't manage more work in progress, then we won't meet our goals."

My response? "If that's reality, wouldn't you want to know that sooner rather than later?"

If someone other than the people doing the work attempts to set a WIP limit for the people doing the work, it will inevitably be based on wishful thinking. A leader may wish the team would accept a WIP limit of 10 because that's what they think is necessary to get the work done. They may not want to accept the reality that whenever that team goes above a WIP of five, quality starts to suffer. But a WIP limit of five does not mean that the team will be limited in their overall performance. It does mean that they will focus on getting done before starting more work.

So, if it's not the leader's job to define a team's work in progress limit, what *is* the job of a leader when it comes to flow?

Your job is to prioritize outcomes.

3. Prioritize: The Verb

RECENTLY, I LED A SESSION with a group of senior leaders who were working through an organizational design plan for making active progress on their strategic priorities. We had already identified that they had about 40 people who could form four persistent teams that would work together for the next year.

This meant real constraint (i.e., boundaries) on how they would work. No individual capacity management matrix allowed.

I gave them an assignment to prioritize their strategic initiatives alongside their "business as usual" efforts for the next 12 to 18 months. They were excited to share that, even though the homework was challenging, they had succeeded in prioritizing their initiatives. They shared a spreadsheet that outlined a high-level overview.

They had initiatives "prioritized" into groups: High-Critical, High-Essential, High, and Medium-High. Within each category, they had two to four big items. When I asked them what their number one priority was, a smart-but-overwhelmed leader told me, "All of the 'High' categories are number ones."

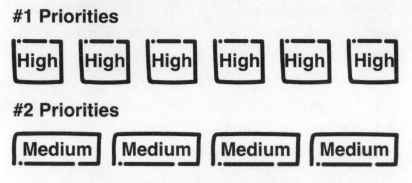

#1 Priorities

High High High High High High

#2 Priorities

Medium Medium Medium Medium

Declaring importance is not the same as PRIORITIZING.

Gently and with a great deal of empathy, I broke the news to them that they had, in fact, not prioritized their work. The initiatives they were trying to deliver in the coming year were complex, and they were right that everything they were working on was of critical importance to the organization. But they had not done the work of prioritization. They still didn't have priorities in place—they just had a differently categorized list.

You might be reading this right now and thinking, "Yeah, but... everything we're working on *is* important!"

And it might be.

You can say no to a thousand objectives and what you are left with may still, in fact, all be important.

If you're an organization looking to get out of regulatory over-sight, like my clients above, you can't just put a pin in something until things slow down because they never actually do. If you lead a social services organization, real people with real needs are likely on the other side of every item on your "to-do" list.

You have an abundance of important work to do. You almost certainly have more important things to do than you have time, money, or people to do them. Those constraints do not make the work any less important.

My point here is not that you need to start doing less, because less isn't an option if the work matters. This isn't about asking, "What do we get rid of?" so much as, "How do we work better within the reality that there is an abundance of important work?" (Though one frequent outcome of making all the work visible on a flow board is that you start to see work that doesn't actually add much value. Say no to those things every time you can.)

You know by now that you can't do everything at the same time. The cost is too great. Limits are real whether we acknowledge them or not.

LEADING IN REALITY

Macro to Micro Lens

I ALWAYS START WITH A macro to micro lens. What is the en-terprise "win" in the landscape we are and *will be* operating in, and then what does my team need to deliver? We each have a role to play, so aligning my intent and objectives is critical. I then take my leadership through a process where we evaluate options on where to play and how to win. As a leader, it is my job to create an environment where we can share, debate, and decide. Execution of strategy and the appropriate investment in the priorities are critical. We engage in an active discussion on our key performance indicators (both leading and lagging). From there, we identify what we need to achieve month by month with clear accountability for each item. We review this when we meet monthly and focus on the yellow and red items that aren't on track. We use the collective wisdom of the team to problem solve. The hardest thing to do is to talk about what we are going to stop doing in order to achieve our objectives. Since there are always new ideas or projects that come in over the year, there has to be a prioritization process that takes into account the real capacity of the organization.

It is also critical to communicate with the rest of the organization and make the linkage clear between the priorities and what they do every day.

—Veena Lakkundi, Senior Vice President, Chief Strategy Officer and Technology Transformation, 3M[66]

It's similar to acknowledging that every cup of water you have is important, but that you can't juggle them all at the same time. If you do, you'll spend most of your capacity focusing on not spilling something instead of focusing on carrying the water.

To be clear, the goal here is not to single-task or to only have a single initiative. If you're a big organization (or even just a busy leader), you're always going to have multiple priorities. That's why you must figure out your WIP limit: how many outcomes can you (or your ecosystem) effectively pursue at the same time without flooding and leading to bottlenecks and unwanted costs?

It may be one. You may be at a small organization, or you may have a goal so monumental that one big priority at a time is absolutely the correct work in progress limit.

It might be 10. If you have 10 teams available, it's not unreasonable to have each of them working on a different outcome.

At the same time, if those teams have a lot of interdependencies or you are short on time to accomplish that goal, as was the case with Marta's company, eight might be a more appropriate work in progress limit because you need some teams to work on a shared outcome. If you lead a global manufacturing business with a supply chain that crosses international borders, you might thoughtfully consider different WIP limits for different areas in your organizational ecosystem.

Next comes the important step of prioritizing, choosing which of the many important things to get done next. It's not about prioritizing in spite of everything being important. It's about prioritizing *because* everything is important.

The truth is, you cannot complete the amount of work you need to accomplish without prioritizing and working within your work in progress limit. And even if you attempt to do so, you can't run at that pace forever because people will eventually burn out and performance will suffer.

This is why any attempt to work without a WIP limit and prioritization results in heavy losses.

The Allure of Pushing vs. the Power of Pulling

IF THERE ARE NO LIMITS to how many priorities you can have in progress at the same time or how many ways you can divide your capacity into percentages, then every single time a new idea, opportunity, or problem emerges, it gets pushed into the river and someone gets started on it.

Prioritizing is hard. I'll say it again. It's perhaps one of the hardest responsibilities of a leader. And if there are no limits on work in progress, then there is not a compelling reason to do the hard work of prioritizing.

But...

If you embrace the discipline of a WIP limit, everything changes. If your organization has a work in progress limit of 10 and you move one of those big 10 priorities to **done**, now you have space for something new.

What new opportunity, feature, or project will you *pull* into the workflow next? What needs to get **done** next? *That is THE performance question.*

This allows you to be in control of the flow. Nothing is going to flood the river in a pull system because you won't let it.

Now you have a compelling reason to do the hard work of prioritizing.

Prioritize your flow of work.

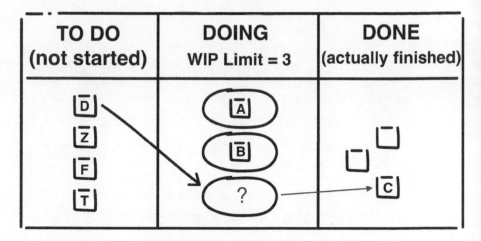

The PERFORMANCE QUESTION: what needs to get done next?

Obstacles Ahead

IF YOU'VE DECIDED TO DO the hard work outlined in this chapter, you should know that you're going to face roadblocks on the way to change.

When you make work visible, limit work in progress, and make prioritization transparent, your backlog of "to-do" goals will inevitably become overwhelming. You will see the weight of all the important work to do. This is the time to stand firm in your leadership.

Obstacle: You Will Want to Increase the Size of Your Boats

YOU MAY BE TEMPTED TO make projects or goals *huge* so that you can still get everything in progress without violating your work in progress limit, but doing so would harm you more than help you. Here's why.

Let's imagine there is now a limit to the number of boats you'll let go down the river at a time before more boats get filled up and sent downstream. When you first start to limit the number of boats and, therefore, the amount of cargo, you'll have a big backlog of stuff waiting. You'll feel the pressure to get it moving down the river.

You may even have some suggest that if you just started using barges instead of boats, you'd be able to fit much more cargo on each boat. That way, you can keep your work in progress limit of 10 but move much more with 10 barges.

This idea has the appearance of good logic, but it crumbles. I call this *clumping*.

If you have 15 new client projects to address, grouping them all into one ginormous bucket and calling it "the new clients project" and rationalizing that it only consumes one of your work in progress buckets is cheating—and you are the one who loses. Well, you and the people who you are still flooding with too much simultaneous work.

Instead, keep the boats and the containers for your goals and objectives small. Ten canoes will navigate a challenging river much better than 10 barges. Instead of playing games with the size of your container, focus on making sure those containers and the people responsible for them have everything they need to work together effectively without impediment.

Obstacle: You Will Want to Stop When It Doesn't Work Right Away

COMMITTING TO VISUALIZING WORK, SETTING WIP limits, and prioritizing is simple, but it is not easy. Furthermore, making your work visible and limiting how much your organization pursues at the same time will lead to radical transparency—transparency that will most definitely be uncomfortable and probably painful at times.

But you won't be flooding.

You may feel as if you've set everything on fire, though. One work in progress limit evangelist famously said, "Any time you create a pull system, it will crash and burn within a short time. There will be glowing and charred pieces [everywhere]." But those pieces will tell you exactly what you need to work on, where to put your focus so that, in your next iteration, your work in progress limit is more useful.[67]

When the fire gets hot, many around you will say that this approach "will never work here." Many people are so uncomfortable with the incongruence between reality and the promises of modern management that they invest heavily in finding reasons to disprove observable reality. Humans are hardwired to do this—it's yet another cognitive bias, the *confirmation bias.* In the journal article "The case for motivated reasoning," Ziva Kunda wrote, "We give special weight to information that allows us to come to the conclusion we want to reach."[68]

Transparency means there is no room for hiding. There is no room for ego. There is no room for incompetence. There is no room for waste.

That is uncomfortable. So uncomfortable that, when the actions that enable flow expose other problems in your organization, many will choose to blame the new actions instead of searching for the root causes.

Recognize confirmation bias when it starts to happen, and search for ways to iterate forward instead of reverting to the old patterns of doing everything at the same time.

There Are No Best Practices

THE PEOPLE WHO WORK AT your organization are part of a wonderfully unique ecosystem—an ecosystem that is not the same as the ecosystem in the organization across town. Knowing this, understand that there are no best practices that will work the same in every organization. None. It's a waste of time to search for the best practice.

We'll talk more about this in Chapter 9, but it's important for you to know now that this is why I'm not giving you a recipe to follow for magic success. There is no magic. Just science.

Your ecosystem is unique, but the principles of human brain science and collaboration are universal. Every human brain can do one executive function at a time. There are real boundaries that exist when groups of humans work together. Your time and energy will be much better spent learning how to work within the wisdom of human biology that has evolved over millions of years instead of working against it.

Keep going. Make a change. Iterate. And keep learning.

Follow the Leader

THE MOST POWERFUL, FASTEST, AND longest-lasting organizational transformation that I have ever been part of happened in a company of 5,000 employees. The executive C-Suite leaders held themselves accountable for making transformational changes to the way the company was organized and the way work was prioritized.

There was no handoff to a change management team. There were no programs established. The executive team simply started by changing the way they worked together and became extremely transparent about it along the way.

They learned and modeled the principles of flow themselves before they asked anyone else to do it. They created a large flow board with the three columns "to do," "doing," "done." They used this board to track their work together as a leadership team before they tried to roll it out to include all the priorities and objectives of the enterprise.

The CEO placed this board near the main employee entrance of the building, and the leadership team began having short daily huddles right in front of the board. These huddles were only for the executive leadership team to participate in, but anyone was welcome to linger in the atrium to observe. Updates to the board were published on the company's intranet site daily.

Each C-Suite leader hosted monthly town hall meetings with their part of the organization to share what they were doing, answer questions about priorities, and explain what they were learning. One of the most remarkable things they shared was that the idea for this came from observing how one of their product teams was using a similar board to manage team-level work.

Along the way, the executive team started adding strategic objectives to the board. Everyone knew when the leadership team was kicking off their annual strategic planning process and that they were going to do it differently than in years past. When changes to funding happened, it wasn't a surprise since that objective had been on the board for months before it finally made it into the "doing" column.

And when one executive formally asked her divisions to start using a flow board in the same way, she found that over half of the area was already using some sort of visual management board and experimenting with work in progress limits. Why? Because they'd seen it on full display for months. Within a year of the executive team making their flow board visible, using a work in progress limit, and being explicit about prioritization for their own work, they had a portfolio-wide view of the flow of work in every area of the company.

They ended the flood forever.

Your organization can too—but it has to start with you. It happens when you understand, accept, and take responsibility for the change you're about to ask of everyone. And it gets easier and better when you're transparent about the practice you're using for yourself.

After you've created flow for yourself, you'll be ready to make your organization's work visible, set a WIP limit, and prioritize.

You too can end the flood forever.

CHAPTER SIX

YOU CAN BE MORE PRODUCTIVE THAN YOU REALIZE

I KICKED OFF MY BOOK-WRITING endeavor with a writing sprint. I went to the beach with a suitcase full of sticky notes. I made sure to stay in a room with a big blank wall and a view of the ocean. I was in my total happy place.

I created a sprint week because I knew I would need focus to do the work—and it was effective. By the end of the week, I had a wave of momentum and was on track to wrap up my book in the spring of 2020.

But then I came home to a global pandemic spreading across the U.S.

Within two weeks, my community was in crisis, my kids were home from school, and I had to temporarily shutter our family business. At the same time, my clients needed me more than ever, so I was rapidly learning new skills as a virtual speaker and facilitator to keep my consulting practice up and running.

And I was still trying to get up to write for the first few hours every day. I'd been told by several successful authors that it's important to stick to a writing routine. But despite my best effort, I wasn't keeping pace with my goal.

I heaped a healthy dose of regret and guilt onto everything else because I wasn't making progress on my book. I *knew* there were good reasons for that, but I still suspected that if I were a true high-performer (which I liked to believe that I was), I should be able to make it happen. I wondered if *I* was the problem.

The real problem? I was disconnecting my measure of productivity from the outcomes I was after.

Productivity without outcomes is not real productivity.

I had an abundance of priorities: all real, all important, all immediate. I had even done the hard work of rank prioritizing—and book writing landed about #5 on my list. Yet I was still beating myself up for not being productive enough. In reality, I had taken my one whole human self and attempted to divide my daily time between all the things that needed my full attention.

In my plan, book writing was one of my five top priorities. On my calendar, it had been assigned about 20% of my workday, but in reality, the writing was getting approximately 0% of my brain space—except for the brain space where I was feeling guilty about not getting more done on the book.

The sirens of modern management and the machine paradigm would have liked me to believe that if I am using all my energy, time, and resources getting items on my task list done, I am being highly productive. But even though I was checking off my writing time every day, I wasn't moving forward.

The insidious thinking goes, "If I can't make progress on my book every day, I am not being productive enough." However, my actual goal wasn't to make progress every single day. My real goal, the real outcome I was after, was to meet my deadlines so that I could publish on time.

Therefore, *publishing the book* was the real outcome. Making progress toward that outcome was the actual measure of my productivity, however it happened.

Effective productivity must be connected to measures of success, and measures of success are highly contextual.

For example, one of my friend's objectives is to write every day so she can build a writing habit. I was not interested in a writing habit; I was interested in getting my book out into the world. Daily writing time wasn't going to get me there, not during a pandemic.

I needed more writing sprints.

This book was written one sprint at a time. I didn't measure productivity by hours of writing, but rather by micro-outcomes (i.e., chapters completed). Every chapter done got me closer to my goal of publishing. And my real, most important measure of productivity will be based on what happens after *you* finish reading. That's how I'll measure my actual performance.

The Problem with Productivity

IN THIS CHAPTER, WE WILL be discussing why and how implementing flow principles will open up the possibility of exponential performance. And because we often think that the highest performers must choose work over their well-being, I want to make it very clear that principles of flow can lead to exceptional performance without anyone having to sacrifice their happiness and well-being.

For much of my life, I conflated productivity with performance. I've learned over the years that I'm not alone. Because of those culturally entrenched illusions we covered back in Chapter 2, many of us simply get performance wrong. It happens because we tend to pay attention to the wrong things, in two significant ways:

1. Outputs vs. Outcomes

2. Capacity Utilization vs. Flow

For flow to enable higher performance in your organizational ecosystem, you will have to pay more attention to the items on the right: Outcomes and Flow. If the misconceptions of performance are widespread in your organization, you'll need to directly confront this mindset shift.

Problem #1: Outputs vs. Outcomes

Outputs are the effort you exert and are entirely within your control to produce. Outcomes are the result of your effort, and they represent impact and value to your customers and stakeholders.

In the world of social impact evaluation, leaders have long known the difference between outputs and outcomes, but in the world of corporations and technology-driven companies, it's a significant shift in focus.

Look at it this way. Output equals...

→ Building a bridge.

→ Hanging a picture frame on the wall.

→ Paddling hard in a boat.

Whereas outcome equals...

→ People walking safely across the bridge.

→ Smiling every time you see the happy family photo.

→ And the outcome of paddling hard? *It depends.*

Outputs	Outcomes
the activity	the result

building a bridge

getting safely across the river

hanging a frame

smiling at the family photo

paddling hard in the kayak

reaching the finish line

enjoying the scenery

Outcomes are entirely contextual depending on the value you want to create. Perhaps the value in paddling hard in a boat is enjoying more of the scenery on the river. Perhaps the value is in delivering cargo to people waiting downstream. Perhaps the value is to get exercise.

Productivity and outcomes depend on knowing *why* you are doing the work. Knowing why and what the outcome needs to be is entirely a leadership responsibility.

In other words, output equals...

→ Writing 40,000 words.

→ Releasing 10 new features in your mobile app.

→ Building a new medical clinic.

Whereas outcome equals...

→ Readers learning something meaningful.

→ Users finding those features useful enough that they will pay for them.

→ Improving the health of community members.

Outputs answer the question, *How will we do it?*
Outcomes answer the question, *Why does this matter?*

A *useful* outcome will also answer the question, *How will we know when to celebrate?* In other words, it will pass the infamous Champagne Test, which you'll recall means the criteria will be clear enough that everyone will know exactly when it's time to pop the bottle open and celebrate.

It doesn't matter how many bridges are built if no one is able to cross safely to the other side. It doesn't matter how many new clinics are built if health and well-being don't improve. (Unless the goal is to make as much money as possible; then people's health can be taken out of the equation. Motive matters too.)

Because there is an abundance of creative ideas to pursue and problems to solve, you can't afford to spend all your time and money and people on being busy. Much like we discussed in Chapter 2, treading water won't get you anywhere, but it consumes at least as much energy as swimming forward.

If all anyone is doing is expending energy (which you most certainly will be if your organization is flooded with competing priorities), you may have profitable quarters, but you will mistake being busy for being productive and settle for mediocre outcomes—mediocre outcomes that will most certainly impact your quarterly results down the line. Ultimately, your impact and your growth will be limited by basic math.

So first, get clear about your outcomes. Then change how you measure your progress.

This brings us to problem #2.

Problem #2: Capacity Utilization vs. Flow

IN 2016, THE USA WOMEN'S Olympic track and field team competed in the final 4 × 400 relay, defending their Olympic title against Jamaica, the reigning world champions.

In a 4 × 400 relay race, four runners take turns running laps around the track with a baton. The winning team gets the baton across the finish line first while following all the meticulous rules about when and where runners exchange the baton.

Want to know who will win every time?

All you have to do is watch the baton. The winning team is the group of runners that moves the baton most effectively.

The Olympic relay race is a remnant of how messages traveled in ancient Greece. Runners would station at their outposts, waiting to receive a message and then ferry it to the next outpost. The goal was to move the message, *quickly*. In the context of sports, the message turned into a baton, and the modern relay race was born.

When I was watching this race in the 2016 games, I couldn't help but watch the waiting runners. In a team of four, only one person is running at a time. Everyone else is in some stage of waiting. No one on the field appears bothered by this. Performance and ultimate success are measured by how quickly runners move the baton. Every coach, runner, and fan understand this.

But if managers were coaches, they would probably be paying more attention to the waiting runners, just like I was, and might be saying, "What a waste of time to have all those runners just standing around," or "I'm paying these runners to run, not to watch," and maybe, "We have some free capacity here, let's work on our utilization rate. Let's have relay team members throw discus when they aren't running."

No more waiting around. Time to work on discus.

Much better athlete utilization rate.

If Olympic coaches thought like modern management.

The machine paradigm tells you and everyone else to watch the runners, to measure productivity by individual utilization. *How busy is everyone? What percentage of hours in the day are they doing their job? Could they take on some more work?*

In a team of elite Olympic athletes, you can immediately identify the problems with trying to get 100% capacity utilization from individual relay runners. A person doesn't simply throw a discus while they are waiting to run their lap in the relay.

Even if that person was as good at discus as they were at running, you wouldn't have them do both in the same afternoon. The opportunity cost is too great. The transition is expensive: the warmup needed for both, the lack of focus on either event, the energy expended throwing discus that is no longer available for running.

There would be a huge context-switching tax that no competitive athlete or coach would want to pay. Yes, you may have reduced the amount of time the relay runners spent standing around, but at the cost of a slower-moving baton.

Runner utilization is the wrong measure of productivity—it's limiting, and it would keep Olympic runners from ever winning a race. In the same way, measuring productivity by utilization is limiting your organization too.

Instead of measuring productivity by how full everyone's capacity is, look at productivity like a relay race, measuring by how work flows from start to finish within your organization. You can measure flow by assessing *cycle time*, the amount of time it takes for an idea to turn into something usable and done.

Most organizations don't measure this, and most leaders don't know the answers to basic cycle time questions:

→ Do you know what your average cycle time is for projects or new features or initiatives?

→ While there is certainly going to be variability, can you find any patterns?

But you probably *do* feel the slow cycle that exists in a flooded organization:

→ Do new ideas move fast through planning and design, only to get stuck waiting for another team down the line to get to work?

→ Do policy changes take a long time to work their way through endless discussion because it's unclear who gets to make the decision?

→ Are you quick to start planning new programs, only to have them languish in progress forever because no one has time to follow through on the action items?

You will be able to better understand your cycle time and improve it when you make the flow visible. Follow the flow principles in Chapter 5 and you will start to see how much time and effort it takes to go from idea to value and obtain real productivity—productivity that gets you from idea to value with less time and effort, not more.

And you know what predictably slows down cycle time more than anything else? Work in progress that exceeds your WIP limits.

Effective Matters More Than Efficient

AN ECOSYSTEM VIEW OF YOUR organization requires that you pay attention to the parts, the whole, and the greater whole.

Efficiency is a metric that focuses only on each individual part. Efficiency is caring only about how fast each member of the team is running.

Effectiveness is paying attention to how fast the baton is moving. The winners aren't the fastest runners. The winning team is filled with the fastest runners who *also* effectively transfer the baton.

Instead of pursuing efficiency, pursue effectiveness.

Effectiveness = efficiency + outcomes

I live in the heart of a big city. In my neighborhood, there are no attached garages, so I park on the street in front of our house. It's a long walk from the car to my kitchen, and for that reason, I am famous in my family for wanting to make as few trips from the car to the house as possible when I return from a grocery run.

Here's the thing: It might *feel* more efficient for me to pile as many bags of groceries as possible into my arms, but it's not the most effective thing to do. More often than not, I waste a tremendous amount of time shimmying the bags up my arm, fiddling with my keys, and occasionally dropping a bag or two. It might feel like I'm being more productive because of how much I'm struggling, but that's simply not true.

The effective thing to do—the thing that would be efficient *and* yield better outcomes—would be for me to grab a reasonable number of bags, drop them inside, and then come back for more. No broken eggs, no problem.

LEADING IN REALITY

Focus on One Fix at a Time

I CREATE A ROADMAP BY quarter with my team. When all the little asks are hitting the team, we vet them against the roadmap. We have made huge gains in productivity by doing this. How can we fix the processes that we need to manage the day-to-day work of HR? Instead of putting Band-Aids on the sub-processes that we get complaints on, we funnel those into a backlog and focus on fixing one process at a time. We are always talking about operational versus strategic work. We'll never be strategic if we can't manage the day-to-day operations, and a roadmap helps us make progress every day toward that end goal. It frees up the time we need to be more strategic partners.

—Carolyn Ramsey, Senior Director, Talent, Digi-Key[69]

The Shockingly Simple Way to Get More Done

IMAGINE YOUR GROUP HAS THREE important initiatives: A, B, and C. They are *all* important and your stakeholders want to see progress, so you get to work right away.

Super important initiatives must be completed
by the end of the year. We have 6 months.

What typically happens is that you start A, B, and C, then a new idea or priority emerges, and you start that too because, "Hey, it's important!" Stakeholders want to see progress, and so does everyone else.

However, the appearance of progress comes with a trade-off: the hidden flooding tax of a group of people stuck in the whirlpool of context switching. And when your work isn't physically visible, it's nearly impossible to see the flooding tax.

How many things are you doing at any given time? How many projects, initiatives, and strategic priorities are you focusing on? When your progress is visible, you can answer that question quickly. When it's visible, you can see the bottlenecks and constraints. When it's visible, you can see the otherwise hidden cost of too much work in progress.

But when work in progress is not readily visible, it's nearly impossible to recognize the heavy losses of organizational multitasking.

Real Productivity and Exponential Math

FOR EASY MATH, LET'S SAY that in this current environment of constant flooding, you have an average project cycle time of six months, meaning it takes six months to go from idea to final execution. You get the value of each effort when it's done.

But the math isn't straightforward. Finishing tasks is slowed down by starting new tasks. For every new task you start, the time it takes to finish an in-progress task increases.

What if you had a work in progress limit of one? Instead of starting all three new things, you start just the first one. In our example, with a WIP limit of one, it takes two months to complete effort A, and then you get the value from whatever that project is.

After you start effort B, it takes two months of active work to complete. From the moment you knew it was a priority until you are getting value from the work, it has now been four months.

Now you can start C. With all that focus, C is also finished in two months of active work. And even though you waited four months to start that last project, it still only took six months of total time to finish three projects instead of one.

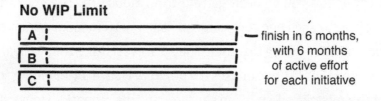

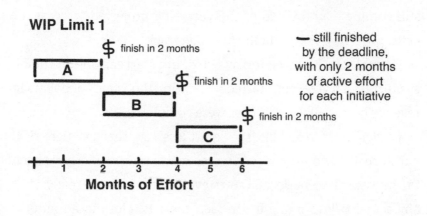

Here's another way to look at the relationship between work in progress and performance. Let's say you are a real estate developer who wants to build three new houses, with the goal of renting the houses when they are done. There is no revenue until they are complete and rented. There's no time to waste; you need to get started right away.

There's two ways you could go about this. If your crew works on those three houses simultaneously, it might take them a year to finish all of them. That's a full year until you can start getting a return on your investment.

Alternatively, if your crew establishes a WIP limit of one and focuses on getting one house built at a time, your first house will likely be done in three to four months. House #1 gets rented out. Meanwhile, the crew starts on House #2. Three to four months later, House #2 starts bringing in rental income, in addition to the income that you've been getting from House #1. The crew, having just finished two complete builds, has a tremendous amount of experience working together. They use everything they've learned building the first two houses to complete House #3, avoiding some of the mistakes they made early on. In this scenario, House #3 is still complete by the end of the year. The projected forecast for getting all three houses built stayed on track.

Unlike in the first scenario, which didn't start earning you money until after a year, you started generating thousands of dollars in revenue before all three houses were completed.

Leaders tend to feel like the "start less" approach is high-risk, but in reality, no project was worse off than it would have been in the typical scenario of "start everything." There really isn't any actual risk to trying it—in fact, there is a lot more room for potential benefit.

When one part of the ecosystem improves without harming any other part of the ecosystem, it's called a *Pareto effect*, named after Italian economist Vilfredo Pareto, who was fascinated by the intersection of sociology and economy.

Pareto also demonstrated another useful economic pattern: *the Pareto principle*, where, in many cases, 20% of all effort results in 80% of the value. The reverse of this principle is that 80% of effort only adds 20% of value.[70] This is a pattern, not a scientific law, so it's the principle here that matters most. Some work yields outsized results, while other work is time consuming and low value.

Doesn't it sound fantastic to focus on the smaller amount of work that will add the greatest value? The organizations that accomplish more of their outcomes are the ones that are relentlessly applying the 80-20 principle. They deliver on more outcomes because they are actually doing less work for each one. They are treading less water. This doesn't make them lazy; it makes them effective. And with all the additional time that they aren't spending on low-value work or context switching, they can actually get more valuable work done.

The fear we often have is that if we put a work in progress limit in place, we'll get less done. But WIP limits actually have the opposite effect. WIP limits increase productivity over time. In our simple example of using a WIP limit of one, the average project completion time went from six months to four months!

Similarly, if you have a team of people focused on those three projects and that team costs $200,000/month to employ, you just reduced your overall cost to deliver those three new features by 33%, or $400,000... *and* delivered an average of two months ahead of schedule, just by introducing a WIP limit.

Now, you may be thinking, "That's nice, but we'll never have a work in progress limit of one. While the example is pretty, my organization is way more complex."

A work in progress limit of one might be unrealistic for an entire organization. That's okay. However, the more complex your organization, the more true and powerful the relationship between work in progress limits and productivity. The reality is your organization does have a work in progress limit—a line beyond which quality suffers, performance diminishes, and people start to burnout. Your job is to figure out what it is and work with it, not against it.

The principle of WIP limits scales up. While a work in progress limit of one might not work as a company-wide limit, it might very well be the perfect limit for a single team.

One company I worked with had a portfolio of products that included over 50 technology teams. When I first met the group of executive leaders, they had over 250 regulatory changes stuck as work in progress, with another 57 slated to kick off in the next few weeks. Every single one of these items had to be solved by December 1 of that year or the company would be out of compliance and unable to operate their business in Europe.

It was April 25. They had completed only two changes to date.

There were over 100 project managers deployed to coordinate the work between teams and provide status updates to leaders. Not a single leader I spoke with was confident that they would meet their deadlines.

In a one-on-one conversation after a particularly stressful meeting, one of the executives confided to me that she had never felt so out of control as a leader.

This was a relatively healthy organization. The leaders were invested in empowering their teams and creating a great work environment, but they were under an intense amount of pressure to meet deadlines outside of their control. And that pressure was leading to alarming behaviors.

Everyone was working as hard as they could and putting in long hours daily. They hoped and prayed that everything would be done by the deadline but hopes and prayers aren't a solid strategy. They needed a different way to manage the flow of work toward their goal.

To get there, the leadership team needed to embrace their shared responsibility for meeting the December 1 deadline.

One spring day, the leadership group decided to do the following five things differently:

1. **They put all 307 regulatory change projects on a flow board.** They also added in everything else that was in the mix: bugs that needed to be fixed, new features that got started at the beginning of the year, general maintenance, etc. It wasn't pretty, but at least they knew exactly what their reality was. Visualizing the work revealed that with their current cycle time, if nothing else unexpected happened, they would likely get through 55% of their backlog before their December 1 deadline. This was bad, but reality was now on the table—and it's easier to solve problems in reality rather than in hopes and dreams.

2. **They decided on an organization-wide WIP limit of 50.** No more than one issue per team at a time. They worked with their teams to determine which 50 issues should stay in progress and which ones needed to return to the backlog of

"to do" and wait until the WIP limit dropped below 50. This allowed leaders and teams to know exactly where to focus and significantly reduced the flooding tax they had been paying for rampant organizational multitasking.

3. **They rank-ordered every single item according to customer use area.** Their rationale was that if they were unable to get the regulatory changes finished by the deadline, then they should group the issues according to customer needs so that critical customer-facing functions would remain available, even if some areas of their business had to go offline. This leadership team hoped that they wouldn't have to go offline anywhere, but grouping efforts by customer needs enabled them to focus on value and manage the risks. They now had the information they needed to have trade-off conversations if necessary.

4. **They reorganized their teams into customer groups.** Using an ecosystem lens, they did a similar exercise to what Buurt-zorg did. They took a high-level view of how the projects were overlapping with teams, and what they saw instantly explained the headache that so many people were feeling. The number of dependencies between teams created a complicated web of communication and coordination pathways that weren't showing up on the roadmaps but represented very real costs in time and money. By organizing groups of teams into customer areas, they were able to reduce the complexity of those dependencies, create even more focus, and make it easier to execute from start to finish.

The path to deliver on paper

(A)→(B)→(C)→(D)→(E)→(F)→★

The path to deliver in reality

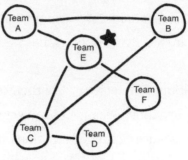

Reorganized by customer need, the path to deliver was simplified

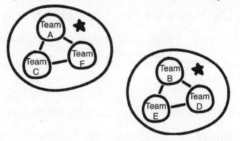

They started a coordinated daily huddle practice. Every morning, each team had a short huddle. One person from each team then joined their customer-area huddle to share any issues that were raised in the team huddle. Finally, each customer-area team of teams sent a representative to the executive leadership team huddle to bring up any issues or blockers that remained unresolved.

By 10 a.m. every day, the leadership team knew exactly what was going well and what impediments were putting the team's goals at risk. As teams were accomplishing small goals each week and focusing on continuous improvement, their ideas and blockers were flowing straight to the leadership group for action. Those issues went on the leadership group's own flow board, and while teams were working hard to address each regulatory change, leaders were working hard to solve problems that were slowing down flow.

The result?

The organization completed 95% of their regulatory changes by the December 1 deadline. Because of the way they prioritized the work, their highest-use customer functions stayed online and uninterrupted. They did have to take one function offline.

However, in analyzing the impact of not offering that particular functionality, they realized that only a small percentage of their customers used the feature, and those that did only did so occasionally. The leader for that product area made the decision to retire that feature instead of investing more time and money into its upkeep, leaving them with more to invest in other higher-value items.

This is what is possible when you stop relying on the basic math of a machine paradigm and embrace the exponential math of an ecosystem paradigm where an outcome greater than the sum of each part is possible.

Courage Will Be Necessary

EMBRACING THE BOUNDARIES OF WIP limits for the first time will feel like you are asking everyone in your organization to move to Mars with you. Many people will resist. They will find the perceived risk too great.

For people who have been working and leading in a flooding organization, the overwork and overwhelm seem normal. Busyness as a substitute for productivity, while exhausting, is comfortable. Basic math where an organization is broken down into its component parts and optimized is familiar, and starting all important work right away seems like the right thing to do.

Making work visible, committing to a work in progress limit, and implementing radical prioritization will feel too risky. What if the flood doesn't stop? What if you are wrong about the way human brains work?

LEADING IN REALITY

My Personal WIP Limit

THE ONLY CONSTANT WE HAVE is change. I know that's become kind of a cliché statement, but it's true. It's easy to get overwhelmed by the number of things that land on my to-do list. I used to look at my to-do list as "I have these twenty things that have to get done," and then something would change, and I'd have 10 more things added to my list. Then something else would come up, and something else. I'd get tired just looking at the growing list. But as I started to understand how work in progress limits enable focus, my entire approach changed.

Now I look at my to-do list each week with clear focus. What needs to be *done* by the end of the week? Given that, what are the three things I need to accomplish today?

I focus on the top of my to-do list because it's likely that items #10 to #20 will change before my WIP limit allows me to address them. If midday an item that was #10 on my list suddenly becomes more critical, then it might become one of the three things I need to get done. I don't suddenly have four things to prioritize; my top three just change. My work in progress limit keeps me focused so that I can do what's most important for my team.

I know that things are going to change in my day and in my week, but I still start with a plan so that when something changes, I know how to adjust. I never tackle things in the order that they come at me because they don't all have the same level of importance.

Getting comfortable with my own personal WIP limit has forced me to dig deeper into what I'm doing so that I understand why each task is important. It helps me prioritize my own time, which is essential. And it helps me model the value of focus for the teams I lead.

—Alan Jechort, Senior Software
Engineering Manager, Blackbaud[71]

The risk will seem too big for some. Some people will fight the shift because they care deeply about the work and are deeply invested in the status quo. Some will fight it because, in the light of transparency, they won't be able to hide that their first priority is short-term profit or their own personal gain.

But reality is reality. And there are very real threats to your success if you continue flooding people, teams, and the entire organization with too many competing priorities at the same time.

So how do you overcome the resistance that you will inevitably encounter?

Practice all the principles together.

You will only experience exponential performance gains if you practice all the principles together. Prioritization without a WIP limit is meaningless. And you won't have a clue what your WIP limit should be unless you first make reality more transparent by visualizing all the work.

You have to be the one to start.

While you can start small, eventually, every part of your organizational ecosystem must operate in the same reality. It won't work to merely tell others what to do. You must model it yourself first and be explicit about why flow matters. Every single person in your organization will need to understand the vision and the goals, and it is your responsibility as a leader to make objectives crystal clear.

Why is changing the way work flows necessary? What outcomes do you want to enable? How will you measure progress? What will you do when it doesn't work exactly as planned the first time around? How will you lead in learning and improving?

Compelling answers to these questions are essential. Otherwise, no one will be willing to change. You must cultivate an ecosystem where improvement is possible, and that starts with modeling the behavior you want to see in everyone else.

Exponentially Higher Performance Is Possible

THE PRINCIPLES OF FLOW CAN be difficult to implement because of fear. Fear of lower performance. Fear of doing less. Fear of losing sight of all the important things your organization needs to get done.

If you take one thing away from this chapter, let it be this: making work visible, setting a WIP limit, and prioritizing is not doing less.

In fact, using the principles of flow can take your organization to a level of achievement it has never seen before.

And your employees will thank you for it. Having been in a world influenced by the machine paradigm for years, they likely have had to sacrifice their humanity for work. Using the principles of flow will make people more satisfied, more focused, and less likely to burn out.

The benefits don't stop there. When your organization gets flow, you will find that other bottlenecks, risks, and problems become easier to spot and resolve. Flow is not actual magic, but it can feel that way because every other problem is instantly easier to solve when you aren't trying to solve it in the middle of a raging river.

CHAPTER SEVEN

OTHER PROBLEMS WILL BECOME EASIER TO SOLVE

WE HAD A MOUSE PROBLEM for a very long time in our 100-year-old house.

We spent years trying to address the issue by diligently and meticulously setting out mousetraps in every entryway we could find. Each time we caught a mouse, we took it far away, dropped it off, and hoped the issue never returned. But it always did.

When we were in the process of rebuilding our back porch, we took the decking off and discovered that we did not have a mouse problem—we had a hole-in-our-foundation problem.

It didn't matter how great we were at trapping mice and removing them because we had an open-door policy. In other words, the mice were just a symptom of the real problem. A symptom we had wasted years trying to cure.

You probably know better than anyone else that there's usually more than just one issue going on at a time in an organization. In reality, it can feel like an unending series of fire after fire—unrelenting, all-consuming, difficult to put out. Not only does the flood of organizational multitasking cause these fires (or at least make them grow bigger), it makes them feel that much more exasperating.

We've already exposed the heaviest loss of organizational multitasking as burnout and lower performance, but the flood is costly in other hidden ways. Over and over again, organizations waste a significant amount of time, money, and energy on solving big problems that are actually just symptoms of the thing that makes them all worse: organizational multitasking.

That's why stopping the flood of organizational multitasking will make every other organizational challenge easier to solve. Enabling flow has a significant impact on three especially hard-to-solve organizational challenges:

→ Inability to Respond to Change

→ Lack of Innovation

→ Culture Problems

Imagine you are back in that boat, navigating a raging, flooding river. Perhaps you discover that a few of the crew members are struggling to communicate as they try to navigate the route. Helping your crew practice new communication skills isn't easy in any circumstance, but it's nearly impossible to do if you are trapped in a raging river, trying to jump between boats while making sure no one is capsizing.

It's easier to work on communication, collaboration, and so many other things when there isn't a crisis. Because these issues are ultimately made worse by organizational multitasking, stopping the flood and creating flow within your organization (by making work visible, creating a WIP limit, and prioritizing) will make the work of solving these problems easier.

Symptom-Driven Problem-Solving

BEFORE WE DIVE INTO THE ways other problems will become easier to solve, we need to understand why symptom-driven problem-solving happens.

Simple cause-and-effect thinking, combined with a culture of busyness, can result in people opting for rapid-fire, short-term solutions for long-term problems. The machine paradigm perpetuates that way of operating.

Humans are drawn to the paradigm of organizations as machines because it appears easier to manage. Less complicated. More comfortable. It's easier to grasp the concept that an organization is made up of a bunch of parts, only connected by the role each part plays in making up the entirety of the group. And if your organization is a machine, you ought to be able to take any complex problem, break it down into its component parts, analyze them until you find the broken piece, replace it, and then put it all back together again. It all works very nicely on paper.

But that's symptom-driven problem-solving at work.

LEADING IN REALITY

Hold It Loosely

Often when I'm trying to figure out why an employee might be underperforming, I realize that underperformance is only a surface symptom of the issue. I might begin by thinking there is underperformance because we've mismatched the employee's skills to what's being asked of them, or we've given them too much autonomy, or any number of reasons. But I find pretty consistently that whatever I first zone in on is usually not what the root issue is. Far more often it is about incentive structures, accountability, or something happening outside of the job.

This is why I find it very important to hold on to my intuitions loosely. I think intuition can be a powerful tool, and I often find myself tuning in to my own mind and body to understand my intuition about a situation. But if I become too attached to those initial stories, I miss out on the opportunity to grow and learn. Holding on to my stories, judgments, and intuition loosely has been critical in helping me avoid altering course too quickly.

—Andrew Means, Senior Director,
Global Impact Data and Analytics, Salesforce[72]

Just like I saw the mice and thought I had a trapping problem, a leader may see low employee retention and think they have a turnover problem. And just like I thought my house could be fixed by catching mice, a leader might think the matter can be fixed by implementing a new employee recruiting program. These practices may help on the surface—similar to how the number of visible mice was reduced because of my traps—but employee-retention goals will never be reached if the underlying problem isn't addressed.

Because it's not readily visible in org charts, it can be more difficult to wrap one's head around the idea that an organization is like an ecosystem, that change can happen in unpredictable ways, and that a small change in one department can have an unintended effect on the entire organization. It may even be a little disconcerting to hear that. And yet it's true.

The more interconnected the ecosystem is, the more we see something called *the butterfly effect*. You may be familiar with the classic example: a butterfly flaps its wings in one part of the world, and the disturbance caused by its wings leads to a hurricane in another part of the world.

The butterfly effect attempts to explain that in an ecosystem, small changes can be transformational, or they may just be small changes with little impact. The challenge is that in a complex system, it's difficult—likely impossible—to predict which small changes will have an outsized impact. Therefore, complex organizational challenges cannot be fully understood with linear cause-and-effect thinking.

Respectively, as psychology and systems theory experts Michael Walcheski and Jim Ollhoff explain, "People don't become systems thinkers because systems thinking is so cool; they do so because they discover that linear thinking won't answer their questions."[73] Unless you go looking for it, it's unlikely that people swirling in the flood will see the many ways in which the organization is interconnected.

Ecosystem leaders recognize the truism that every system is perfectly designed to get the results it gets. If an organization has high turnover or low quality or isn't leading in the marketplace, it's because the way the organizational system functions is somehow designed to enable those results—and, more than likely, one of the design flaws is that the emphasis is on how much work gets started instead of on getting work done. The design that enables starting everything at the same time usually means that competing priorities abound and everyone is trying to divide their time—and themselves—across too many efforts.

As a leader, it's your job to change the design of your organizational system. In other words, it's your job to shape the path of your organizational river so that work flows and people work differently.

When you start shaping your organization to enable flow, you'll find that other problems become easier to solve. Solutions to seemingly intractable problems become much easier to find, implement, and weave into your organization's culture.

Every single problem or opportunity is easier to address when you are no longer dealing with a flood.

Trying to figure out how to improve the construction of your boat to make it nimbler in high winds? Easier to do when you aren't in a raging river. Want to experiment with how many people are actually needed to navigate the boat? Much easier to assess when you aren't hopping back and forth between a dozen boats all day long.

Every single problem or opportunity you have in front of you will be easier to solve in a state of flow and harder to solve in a state of flood. In all of my years working with organizations of every shape, size, and purpose, I have yet to encounter a meaningful scenario where this isn't true. Along the way, I have observed a few persistent themes across organizations, sectors, and leaders.

There are three organizational challenges that become exponentially easier to solve as soon as the flood stops:

1. Responding to Change

2. Innovation

3. Creating a Culture of Inclusion and Equity

The inverse is also true. The flood of organizational multitasking makes these challenges more intense and more damaging and makes the heavy losses that come along with them more devastating. Instead of letting ourselves get sucked into solving the wrong problems or caught in symptoms-based thinking, we must focus on stopping the problem that makes all of them worse.

Responding to Change

CHANGE IS OUR CONSTANT REALITY in the world, in our lives, and in organizations. When it comes to organizations, the more complex the ecosystem is, the more interconnected it is, the more inevitable change is.

When people accept that change is going to affect their organization in unpredictable ways, they often take two different approaches. Some adopt the fortress approach, where they might dive into more planning, analysis, and bureaucracy in an attempt to build huge walls and processes that shield them from change.

On the opposite end of the spectrum is the firefighter approach. When one is overwhelmed by the belief that change is uncontrollable, planning becomes useless. People who favor this approach abandon all attempts to prepare and instead spend their time reacting to every fire that comes their way.

The Fortress Mindset   **The Firefighter Mindset**

Change is bad. Let's avoid it without robust planning.

Change is bad. No sense in planning. Just be ready to react at all times.

Both of these mindsets are exhausting. They waste time, money, and energy.

Management consultant Margaret Wheatley offers a third alternative. She reminds us all that "Uncertainty became our insistent twenty-first-century companion."[74] This is the mindset I encourage you to adopt as well: expect that uncertainty is everywhere and accept that you can't control or predict it all the time.

This is the mindset of *agility*.

Agility is enabled when an organization understands that change will happen, even if they can't predict the specific details of what, when, and where. They may not be able to create a detailed project plan in advance, but they can anticipate that they will need

The Agile Mindset

Change happens. We can plan
for change and respond.

to adapt. Agile organizations plan for change, always.

The principles of flow enable organizations to be more adaptive and nimbler whenever change occurs. When an organization is flooding, it doesn't have any capacity to respond to the inevitable change we've been talking about—even though change *cannot* be stopped.

It's like being on a highway in the middle of rush hour.

Imagine you're in bumper-to-bumper traffic when a bird flies across your window, temporarily distracting you. Because there's no space between the cars on the road, you're left without any room or time to respond accordingly. And when you do react, it's too late: you hit the car ahead of you.

The same thing happens in organizations. If there's no space in the flow of work, any new priorities that arise will immediately cause a backup, and eventually a flood.

The flow principle applied to rush hour traffic would be to create space on the highway, which is what stoplights at on-ramps are designed to do. The same number of cars could be on the highway, but the number of traffic jams is reduced because there's enough space between each of the vehicles. This is the highway version of a work in progress limit.

In an organization, the flow principle of WIP limits plays out similarly. Teams identify a work in progress limit that allows a bit of extra space for future work that will need a rapid response. Think of WIP limits as containers that get filled with work. If you're in a dynamic environment where things change fast, you want to keep one of these containers open for unplanned work or emerging priorities.

While you may not be able to predict what the emerging priority will be, you *can* predict that in most weeks there will be emerging priorities. If you plan for space in your WIP limit to react to the inevitable unplanned work, you will be in a better position to respond and adjust when it comes flowing down the river.

Emerging priority space.
You don't have to know
what the urgent need is
in order to plan capacity for it.

WIP limits enable agility, or responsiveness to change, on two levels: individually and organizationally. At both levels, the principle is the same, but the scale is different. Individually, my WIP limit for consulting engagements is four. I can typically engage with a high level of performance with up to four engagements at a time; however, I only contract with three clients at a time. I do this because I often get invited to participate in interesting collaborations and speaking events. If I fill every single one of my four WIP containers, I don't have time to say "yes" to unexpected invitations. With three clients at a time, my calendar is full, but never packed. This leaves me with room to take on other interesting projects whenever they come my way.

While the WIP limit principle applies to large organizations just as much as it does to individuals, it looks different depending on size, complexity, and nature of work. For example, if there's an organization-wide WIP limit of 10 projects, one per team, you might narrow the WIP limit to nine so one team becomes the responsive group that takes on the urgent, hard-to-plan-for work.

Responding to change is one of the biggest challenges organizations face, but organizations make it even harder by trying to be agile without addressing the problem of too much work in progress. Look at your collective capacity, adjust your organization's WIP limit, and make room for change.

Ending the flood and enabling flow will always make it easier to respond to change. Always.

Innovation

INNOVATION AND CREATIVE THINKING ARE some of the most desired traits in employees and teams. For this reason, thousands of management books are sold every year that offer the "secret" that will make an organization more creative. And despite all of the attention, leaders consistently report a huge deficit of creativity and innovation in their organizations.

Across industries, this phenomenon is often referred to as an *innovation gap*. In my own research, I have found over 5,000 peer-reviewed studies published in the last five years alone that focus on innovation gaps across industries such as technology, farming, hospitality, social services, and so on. A 2019 *Harvard Business Review* article, for example, stated that "innovation has been a top priority—and a top frustration—for leaders. In a more recent McKinsey poll, 84% of global executives reported that innovation was extremely important to their growth strategies, but a staggering 94% were dissatisfied with their organizations' innovation performance."[75]

So, what's going on here? Is it just that people have a finite ability to be creative? Is it that teams need fancier collaboration software? Is it that you need to hire more innovative talent?

It's none of the above. It's not a human nature problem, a recruitment problem, or a motivation problem. The systemic pattern of organizational multitasking is to blame. People are remarkably innovative and capable of creating incredible things for their organizations, but only if they're put in environments that allow them to do that.

And in today's organizational climate, there's little room to be

innovative because people are flooded with the demands of context switching, fractured focus, and pressure from competing priorities. Imagine being told to come up with a unique design for a
boat when you're drowning in a river. Not. Gonna. Happen.

Cognitive scientists will tell you the same thing. It just so
happens that creative thinking is an executive function, like goal
switching and rule activating.[76] As you know, executive functions
can only be performed one at a time, so if an employee is stuck
having to context switch all day, their very human brain is going
to be busy with the tasks of goal shifting and rule activation, not
creative problem-solving.

Furthermore, creativity requires more cognitive effort than
other tasks. Imagine innovation as a uniquely shaped container full
of water that needs to be carried from point A to point B. Because
innovation is a complex process that looks different for everyone,
can't really be nailed down to a formula. It takes more effort to get
the container to its endpoint, making the task a lot harder to complete than if it were a typical jug.

But finding flow can create space for innovation. Harvard business professor and author Adam Grant writes that "innovation =
focused attention + persistent effort."[77] You know what makes focused attention hard? Organizational multitasking.

LEADING IN REALITY

Experiments Aren't Enough

In this age of prioritizing experimentation, prototyping, and speed, it is easy to default to short-term thinking over long-term planning. Get something out next week! Have a bias toward action! Fail early, fail often! These are mantras that have become a rallying cry to get people out of navel-gazing and into action—a valid ambition. But the unintended consequence is that short-term solutions are positioned as "experiments" without sufficient attention to long-term consequences or impact. And often, we end up prioritizing solving *a* problem over solving the *right* problem. By slowing down at the onset and defining the real problem we need to solve, we are able to design experiments that help us come to the right long-term solution.

—Anna Love, CEO & Founder, Stoked[78]

You know what makes focus easier? Finding flow through WIP limits and effective prioritization.

Let's say a person identifies their WIP limit to be 10 because they're doing the same work they have for the last year, which makes it a low cognitive load. But you've just assigned them a different task: to come up with a creative new way to automate a process. All of a sudden, their typical WIP limit of 10 becomes unmanageable because the innovation work they're doing demands more cognitive attention.

Unlike leaving a figurative WIP container open for emerging priorities, innovation work may require a team to reduce their overall WIP limit because of the intense need to focus and persist until new solutions are uncovered.

At the end of the day, it comes down to focus. And innovation requires a lot of it.

A colleague of mine always wrote a mantra at the top of their team's flow board: "*Focus* isn't a four-letter word." It was there to remind them and all their stakeholders that *focus* doesn't mean *lazy* and it's actually a good thing. I've added my own take to their original mantra. Here's my version: "*Focus* isn't a four-letter word, and neither is *prioritize*." In some circles, these words became taboo because in the swirl of high pressure, high stakes, and high multitasking, focus and prioritization sound to some like doing less, but focus and prioritization are critical to innovation, and they are essential to getting more done.

Focusing and prioritizing don't mean *doing less*, they mean *getting more of the right things done*.

White Supremacy in the Workplace

SOME MAY BE SURPRISED TO see white supremacy show up in a book about organizational performance. However, if we're going to get real, honest, and pragmatic about how to actually lead high-performing organizations, then we absolutely need to talk about the insidious ways that organizational multitasking perpetuates inequity in the workplace.

That conversation starts with us understanding why organizational leaders must not merely talk, but actually take serious action to improve diversity, equity, and inclusion. Your organization will not find its true performance potential otherwise.

Prejudice, unconscious bias, and racism are ingrained in our economic systems. They are the reasons why, as of February 2021, there have only been 19 Black CEOs out of 1,800 leaders in the history of the Fortune 500 list.[79] It's also the reason why white applicants with felonies on their records are selected for employment more than Black job applicants who don't have criminal records.[80]

In the article "Why So Many Organizations Stay White," Victor Ray attributes some of these phenomena to "what sociologists refer to as a 'social structure': a resilient distribution of resources that is bigger than any one individual and has sometimes profound implications for our daily lives." He cites inheritance taxes and under-resourced or racially segregated schools as "examples of legally institutionalized social structures."[81]

I believe that it is the responsibility of organizations, and the leaders at the helm of them, to break down these social structures for the betterment of their employees, their organizations, and the world. It's as simple as that.

If you are feeling skeptical that this problem is tied to organizational multitasking, just look at the characteristics of white supremacy work culture outlined in "White Supremacy Culture" by Kenneth Jones and Tema Okun:

→ **Perfectionism:** Focusing on what is inadequate, while minimal resources are invested in learning and continuous improvement. A punitive culture where mistakes are not allowed.

→ **Sense of Urgency:** All work is important and urgent. There is little time for thoughtful decision-making, short-term fixes come with long-term costs, and raising concerns or new ideas is viewed as slowing down the work.

→ **Quantity over Quality:** All resources of the organization are directed toward productivity and measurable outputs; minimal value is placed on emotional intelligence. This is a conflict-avoidant environment.

→ **Document-Driven Communication:** There is no time for conversations. Important discussions and decisions are relegated to agenda-packed meetings, emails, or documents.[82]

See any overlap with characteristics of an organization flooded with too much work in progress?

Jones and Okun write that "Organizations which unconsciously use these characteristics as their norms and standards make it difficult, if not impossible, to open the door to other cultural norms and standards. As a result, many of our organizations, while saying we want to be multicultural, really only allow other people and cultures to come in if they adapt or conform to already existing cultural norms."[83]

These ideas are further expanded on in Aysa Gray's 2019 article "The Bias of 'Professionalism Standards,'" which explains that hiring is too often influenced by "white and Western standards of dress and hairstyle (straightened hair, suits but not saris, and burqa and beard bans in some countries); in speech, accent, word choice, and communication (never show emotion, must sound 'American,' and must speak white standard English); in scrutiny (black employees are monitored more closely and face more penalties as a result); and in attitudes toward timeliness and work style."[84]

Diversity, equity, and inclusion get a lot of buzzword attention in some organizations, but the practices of inclusion and the ultimate goal of equity must permeate deeper than a marketing campaign and effect change beyond HR workshops.

Many leaders want to create a healthier, more equitable culture across their organizations, but their efforts either don't last or never work in the first place. There are many factors at play, but one ever-present reason that cultural change is lagging is symptom-driven solutions (e.g., *Company potlucks on Tuesdays! Inclusion workshops! Team bowling!*).

Although some of these activities can be fun, they will never get down to the root problem: organizational multitasking perpetuates a culture of white supremacy.

Many organizations that emerged in the twentieth century were built by white male leaders, centered in a cultural sea of values that benefited people who were also white and male. Even though many have wanted to move away from these ideals for a very long time, we can't because flooding leaves no room to assess behavior and make change. Norms are perpetuated. Implicit biases go unchecked. Band-Aid solutions like company potlucks are taken. The status quo remains the same.

Organizational multitasking that creates a sense of urgency and focuses on the short-term at the expense of long-term outcomes is damaging because it creates unchecked norms and standards that privilege white supremacy culture. This is damaging to everyone; a constant sense of urgency makes it difficult to take time to engage in continuous improvement and collaboration or thoughtful decision-making, and it leads to a lack of consideration of long-term consequences.

Imagine you're back in that raging river, trying to make sure you and the rest of the boats around you don't capsize. You have zero time to stop and reflect on how you're including everyone's voices, building trust, and ensuring that your organization is not perpetuating a culture that privileges and rewards the way things have always been done.

If a leader's goal is to increase the diversity and inclusion in their organization, but they're not addressing the overwork culture that perpetuates implicit bias and discrimination, then they will never evolve the organization. Instead, implicit norms need to be made explicit, examined, and eliminated so new ways of working together can take their place.

But in order for that hard work to get done, leaders and employees alike need to have enough space to be reflective about their work so that they can actually find ways to change and improve. When they're not given that kind of mental space, they can't create the focus needed to examine how they're working together. Essentially, even if an organization does care about improving equity and rooting out white supremacy thinking, they will be ineffective in doing so as long as a culture of organizational multitasking remains.

It's a mice versus hole-in-the-foundation problem. As long as an organization has a hole in its foundation, it will have an inequitable workplace.

So how do flow principles make cultural change actually possible? By making work visible, limiting work in progress, and being clear on prioritization, you can create time, focus, and energy for teams to have difficult conversations, get to know each other personally, build trust, and identify significant opportunities for learning how to do and be better. You may find that some of your WIP containers need to be dedicated to cultural change in order to ensure that it actually happens.

Ultimately, flow gives you a visual and concrete way to prioritize this hard work of dismantling racism and white supremacy in your organization. Flow is not a panacea, and it won't be the only principle needed to address decades of entrenched and implicit white supremacy in your organizational culture. But I can promise you this: cultural change is nearly impossible while your organization and everyone within it is dealing with a flooding, raging river of multitasking and competing priorities.

The End of Symptom-Driven Problem-Solving

RESPONDING TO CHANGE, A LACK of innovation, and culture problems in the workplace are three persistent challenges that organizations all over the world are actively trying to address.

Of course, there are plenty of additional organizational opportunities and challenges that leaders face. However, I have seen a consistent pattern emerge time and again: leaders treat these challenges as unrelated and spend too much time trying to isolate solutions that merely address symptoms.

Instead, I challenge you to look at the way these problems are connected in your organizational ecosystem. Dig deeper and you'll find that every single one of these problems is only made harder to solve by unending organizational multitasking. Stop the flood, and you will find that it's easier to respond to change, easier to create innovative solutions, and, perhaps most important of all, easier to dismantle racist and inequitable systems that hurt us all.

After all, good work is realized only when people are actually empowered to work well together.

CHAPTER EIGHT

THE FUTURE OF WORK IS PEOPLE

I HAVE TWO KIDS. ONE is eight, the other is six. On a recent Saturday evening, we put on our favorite PG-rated post-apocalyptic movie, *The Mitchells vs. The Machines.*

The night after we first watched it, my kids were a little scared to go to sleep with an Alexa in the house. The next day, one of them asked me, "Your phone talks sometimes, Mom. Can the lady in your phone talk to the other phones? In the movie the phone lady turned evil, but what if they formed an army for good? Do you think phones could get so smart they'd become like phone superheroes?"

My answer? Never. Why, besides the obvious calamity prophesied in the movie we'd just watched?

The future of work is people.

It always has been, and it always will be, no matter what new technology exists or how advanced machine learning becomes. Getting good work done and solving problems that matter is always about how well people work together (just like in *The Mitchells vs. The Machines*).

Looking ahead, spotting new trends (or inventing them), and being future-minded are important parts of leadership. But there is also a dark side to it, and it's not the far-fetched risk that technology will take over and rule the world.

One of the insidious things that keep organizations from creating lasting culture change is an obsession with "the future," as in, what will happen next, when it will happen, and the trending technology that will make it so. People, myself included, quickly become uncomfortable with the uncertainty and complexity of the here and now. We can convince ourselves that "If only we could predict the future, we wouldn't have to spend so much time making meaning of what's happening around us right now." As a result, tremendous amounts of time and energy are invested in anticipating the future.

I can't tell you what will happen next. But I can tell you exactly how the next problems and opportunities of the future will be solved: people. In the future world of work, human beings will be working together to solve complex problems that matter to people.

This is why limiting organizational multitasking and finding flow matters so much. We have to invest in designing organizations and prioritizing work in ways that enable people to do great work because people are the only way that we'll be able to solve future problems.

The Collaborative Worker

IN 1959, MANAGEMENT CONSULTANT PETER Drucker coined the term "knowledge worker" to describe what he saw as the most important skill set in an organization.[85]

He later wrote:

The most valuable assets of the twentieth-century company were its production equipment. The most valuable asset of a twenty-first-century institution, whether business or non-business, will be its knowledge workers and their productivity.[86]

Drucker wasn't wrong, but he wasn't entirely right either. What matters most is not merely one's ability to think, but one's ability to communicate and collaborate with people. It's not individual productivity that matters, it's collective performance. It's not merely our knowledge that drives value, it's our skills of collaboration.

The most valuable asset of the twenty-first-century organization is what I call *the collaborative worker.*

Humans are creative, problem-solving, relational beings who, when given a meaningful goal and a good environment, can create truly astonishing outcomes.

Right now, most organizations are barely realizing the potential that their employees are capable of. Even organizations that hire for collaboration skills hinder what's possible when they exist in an ever-constant flood of organizational multitasking.

The future success of your organization will not be determined by the knowledge and expertise of individuals. The reality is that the best and brightest employees aren't good enough on their own.

You could have the best sales team, the most experienced marketing employees, the smartest engineers. But if these best-in-class people do not communicate well with each other, share knowledge, solve problems together, and collaborate on new ideas, you will never discover the full potential your organization is capable of.

It is the collaboration between people across skill sets and departments that ultimately unlocks the flow of outcomes and the highest levels of performance. This is what it means to have a thriving organizational ecosystem.

Collaboration Is an Executive Function

BUT WHY DOES THE WAY work flows or floods in an organization have such a significant impact on collaboration? The answer goes back to executive functions. Most of the skills required for good collaboration are executive function skills, such as communication, planning, analysis, and perspective shifting. When people are spending their time and energy on context switching, they are not able to simultaneously engage in collaboration functions.

It's a costly trade-off—and that is why the flood of multitasking causes such heavy losses.

The way many organizations are designed ignores the reality of our humanity and the way we're designed to work. The result is a near-constant flood that threatens to drown us all.

The way we fix this is by working *with* our human nature and the organizational ecosystems we inhabit, not against them.

The relationships between people in a group have always fueled the most transformative changes in organizations, communities, economies, and entire ecosystems. For this kind of change to continue, leaders need to empower the collaborative worker.

And it's already starting to happen. Many organizations do recognize the importance of teams and how they work together—by creating cross-disciplinary teams, where people with distinctly different roles, skills, and responsibilities participate in the same team, ultimately accountable, *together*, for the outcomes of the work they do. The result is innovative solutions, better effectiveness and more well-rounded employees. As venture capitalist and Cornell Tech's 2016 Investor-in-Residence Thatcher Bell noted, "Cross-disciplinary teams... are more effective at driving practical results from innovation than teams that are missing [cross-functional expertise]."[87]

Even so, these effective teams are often stifled by organizational multitasking. If an organization is flooding, these teams won't be empowered to collaborate in the ways that would truly lead to higher performance. You could have the most skilled sailing crew and a fleet of well-designed sailboats, but if you put members of the crew in a situation where they have to jump back and forth across sailboats all day long, they won't realize their full potential.

The trick then becomes giving these diverse, highly effective groups space to actually do good work together. You must make an investment in collaboration.

LEADING IN REALITY

Only If We Plan Together

We learned a long time ago at Room & Board that our product launches are more successful if we plan together across all the different departments. Instead of each department working on their own slice of the launch, we come together at the start of every new initiative: product specialists, vendor managers, copywriters, the photo team, web merchants. Everyone who will have even a small part to play is part of the planning from the very beginning.

As long as I've worked at Room & Board, the leadership has been open to listening and learning. From the way we produce our furniture to the way we organize our project teams, we don't take shortcuts; we like to do things the better way. We want to put out the best possible product for our customers. So that means that if it takes longer to get the product or web experience to that place, we will do it.

We value working together and having strong partnerships. All our teams and cross-functional partners have high expectations, and at the same time, we are always thoughtfully working together to improve in sustainable ways. Our culture drives us to look up- and downstream to understand how our work impacts others. Our company is only successful if our collaborations are effective.

—Lisa Knapp, Interactive Project Manager,
Web Customer Experience Team, Room & Board[88]

Team-Based Organizations

SO HOW DO YOU EFFECTIVELY "invest" in collaboration? It all goes back to the principles of flow. By making your work visible, setting work in progress limits, and prioritizing within your organization, you create an environment where people can use their collaborative skills. Then you ensure that people actually get to work together across divisions and departments within your organization. Once you've got boats moving down the river at a sustainable pace, turn your attention to how you assign people to teams for each boat.

Collaborative teams are the way to power a high-performing organization, but for them to be effective, three guidelines must be in practice:

→ **The team must have all of the skills they need to turn an idea into action.** It doesn't work to have all of your skilled navigators together in one boat, the experienced captains together in another boat, and everyone who knows how to build and repair sails off in yet a different boat. It's much more effective to have a navigator, a captain, and a skilled boat-builder working together as a crew that can tackle whatever comes their way. It's the exact same in organizations. Form teams with diverse experience and skills so that they can effectively solve any problem that you prioritize for them to tackle

→ **The team must be in flow.** They need to be transparently managing their work in progress limits so they can focus on getting work that matters done.

→ **The team needs to work together long term.** It takes significant effort and many hours to learn how to collaborate with other people, and each team's pattern of collaboration will be unique. Therefore, splitting up teams and forming new ones for every project will kill collaboration, and the new group will have to start from zero to create their unique pattern of collaboration. A team that builds their collaboration skills together, over time, will be better equipped to spend more of their energy on doing actual work. This is why persistent teams get more done and are generally higher performing.

Many years ago, I worked with a retail company's digital product division to test out the idea of dedicated cross-disciplinary teams in their organization.

This was a radical idea for some the organization's leaders, who were heavily influenced by traditionalist organizational thinking and the machine paradigm. They were skeptical about how diverse teams could be put together and dedicated to working on one thing at a time. One senior director told me, "This will never work. We can't have dedicated teams because there's simply too much work to do."

Because of their doubts, I was only given a little bit to work with: a hastily assembled group of 10 people, all from different disciplines within the division. They were given a challenging problem that some of the organization's top performers had unsuccessfully tried to solve a few times already.

A few months later, the accomplishments of the experimental team were impossible to ignore. Not only did the group find a way to collaborate effectively with one another, but they ended up solving the problem in a creative and effective way—for the first time ever.

When asked about their success, the group pointed to trust they had fostered and their lack of ego; everyone brought different skills and disciplines to the table.

In an enterprise-wide town hall, the division leaders shared with the entire company that they had never had so much transparency into what was happening in the project. They also mentioned how impressed they were by the solution that the team provided and by the fact that everyone upskilled and that the team wanted to continue working together.

Not only did this ragtag-turned-rock-star team get to stay together, they were also given a high-profile opportunity as their next assignment. Soon after, the company formed four other cross-discipline product teams, and over the next two years, they eventually moved all their employees into similarly structured teams.

The Power of Humanity

THE CONCEPT OF PRIORITIZING HUMANS and their collaboration over tools and technology is explored in Malcolm Gladwell's book *Outliers*. He explains the importance of collaboration through a study that looked at the root cause of airline crashes. The study found that the majority of crashes were not due to a breakdown of procedure, but an error in communication or teamwork—*a lack of collaboration*. In Gladwell's words, "The kinds of errors that cause plane crashes are invariably errors of teamwork and communication."[89]

This is startling, but perhaps not shocking. It's yet another example of how much collaboration, or a lack of it, can affect real-world outcomes. You can have your processes, procedures, and policies perfectly defined, but if there's a breakdown in interaction between humans, you will feel the consequences.

Invest in the Collaborative Worker

THE RELATIONSHIPS BETWEEN PEOPLE WORKING together have always fueled the most transformative changes in organizations, communities, economies, and entire ecosystems. For this kind of change to continue, leaders need to empower the *collaborative worker.*

People are the way that high-performing organizations will solve any problem. We don't know what all the problems are going to be in the future, but we do know how they will be solved: through people working how they work best, with focus and collaboration.

The future of work is people. And the most valuable asset of any twenty-first-century organization is the collaborative worker. There's so much we don't know about the future, but as a leader, you can be confident that investing in flow will equip you to navigate it because you will be investing in people working better together. When you create flow, no matter what change is around the corner, your organization will be better positioned to thrive.

CHAPTER NINE

BETTER IS BETTER THAN BEST

AS LEADERS, WE TEND TO love the idea that there is a "best" way to do something.

I am no stranger to this. I find deep comfort in the concept of "best"—getting the best deal, the right answer, the highest quality, the perfect fit—and, of course, piling on the hefty research and analysis to prove to myself and everyone else that I have, in fact, made the best choice.

Exhibit A: The Great Dishwasher Spiral of 2021.

When a dishwasher breaks, many people would head down to their local appliance store to buy a new one that looks decent and doesn't break the bank—but not me. *My* next step was to create a spreadsheet and start researching on Consumer Reports. And Google reviews. And hot takes from Reddit.

The problem with this favorite strategy of mine was that it was a terrible time to be obsessing over a new dishwasher. It was an incredibly busy season for me at work, not to mention that my kids were doing all of their schooling online, from home, pandemic style.

So, weeks went by, then months. I hadn't had time to research what dishwasher would be best for our family, so we hadn't bought one yet. This meant we had spent months as a family of five handwashing everything. We have two small children, run two businesses, and my mom lives with us. The dishwasher problem lasted longer and became bigger than it ever needed to be.

I had been working with a group of product managers at the time who asked me to lead a full-day, put-into-practice workshop on flow. One click into the presentation, I showed a slide with the word "best" crossed out.

I immediately burst out laughing. The irony of what I was teaching quickly sank in.

My husband had spent an hour or two every day washing dishes by hand for the past few months because I didn't have time to find the best dishwasher for my family. *Any* dishwasher would have been better than the "best" dishwasher I was endlessly searching for and didn't have.

That evening, my husband and I went to Home Depot with a budget in mind and an agreement: we'd spend one hour in the store and purchase the best "good enough" dishwasher they had in stock in our price range. It was delivered the following day.

I have never loved an appliance more.

The Danger of Best Practices

WHETHER YOU ARE SHOPPING FOR a dishwasher or leading an organization, there are no universal best practices.

It's disappointing news to hear, but it's the truth.

Leaders often hire consultants like me to teach them how to organize teams, design strategy, and evaluate effectiveness. These are complex, nuanced problems, deeply sensitive to context and culture—and there are no universal solutions to any of them.

In almost every consulting engagement I do, the leaders who hired me eventually wind up asking very earnest questions about best practices.

The concept of best practices makes us *feel* better in a world full of uncertainty. We get lured into believing that if we could find with certainty the "best practices," everything else would take care of itself.

What's the best practice for organizational agility? Leadership de-velopment? Product management? Strategic planning? Customer in-sights? Organizing teams? Keeping talent?

Google any of those questions and you'll find plenty of best practices suggested for each and every challenge. If you want even more certainty, there are plenty of consultants who will provide ready-made best practices for you, for a reassuringly expensive fee.

But in my experience, when leaders search for the elusive best practices, their organizations are often taken far afield from the one thing they actually want: effective progress on import-ant outcomes.

Why?

Because the desire for best practices will send you on a never-ending quest for a thing that doesn't exist. You will waste precious time and resources that could have been spent learning, experimenting, and finding actual better ways of getting work done. Best practices are a harmful myth that keep people in a constant state of analysis, always doubting whether their "best" practices are really best.

Because best practices make you more likely to follow formu-las that were created for someone else, rather than finding re-al-life solutions for your organization. What's best for one orga-nization will never be exactly best for another. Unfortunately, our work is simply never that clean and tidy. Effective outcomes are based on effective ways of working, and effective ways of working are based in a place of reality. The reality is that, while your peo-ple, circumstances, problems, or goals involved may be similar to those of another organization, they aren't identical.

Because the idea of best practices implies there is a ceiling to what is possible. If all an organization cares about is "best," you may find yourself in self-congratulatory complacency once you identify a seeming best practice or you achieve best in market temporarily. That is the machine paradigm at work. It tells us that there is a finite limit to what your organization can do, because there's a finite limit to what a machine can do. In an ecosystem paradigm there is no best, and that is a good thing. Ecosystems are emergent, new ways of evolving are always possible—and therefore, there is no limit as to what is possible.

Ultimately, there are no "best practices," but there are definitively *bad practices*. Organizational multitasking is one of them.

The Two Obstacles You Will Face

AS YOU REJECT THE IDEAS of the machine paradigm, like "best practices," and embrace the potential of the ecosystem paradigm, you're likely to encounter some obstacles along the way. There are two big challenges that almost always get in the way of organizations finding flow and making actual change that sticks.

You'll start to feel like you need to change everything. But *don't*.

Even if you could wave a magic wand and change everything you wanted to all at once, I don't recommend it. You're dealing with a particular set of people in a particular ecosystem that operates in a particular way. Because your organization's ecosystem is complex and you can't predict everything that will happen in the future, changing everything at once is full of risk. It will rob you of the opportunity to learn what works better. Inevitably, you will identify a WIP limit and then learn something significant that leads you to adjust it. Or you will try out one way to make your work visible and find that a better method emerges. You will launch a new collaborative team and find a smoother way for the next team to get started. This is an ecosystem at work.

Instead of making a grand and instantaneous mandate that everyone change everything, start in one area first. This will allow you to apply early learnings to the next area and the one after that. Evolutionary change allows you to find what is going to be most effective for the unique culture of your organization and the people who power it.

The second obstacle you may encounter is the desire for a playbook.

Because cutting back on organizational multitasking is no easy feat, you might feel like you need a checklist to walk you through the exact steps you and everyone else should take. The problem is, there are no formulas or detailed checklists for you because there is no one right way to move forward. There is no best way to do this.

The adjustments you're going to make in your organization will be hard, but you can't shortcut the learning process. The approach your organization takes will need to fit your ecosystem. No one, including me, can tell you what that will look like every step of the way.

Let's see how this can play out with an example. A regional healthcare system brought me in to help them increase their agility as they were rapidly developing technology to enable virtual healthcare. During this time, the CTO wanted to make some massive changes to the way the company was operating, but his peers weren't all on board.

My response was that he couldn't force the change. If he wanted lasting transformation, everyone in the company needed to understand their organizational ecosystem, own the flood caused by their unending pursuit of competing priorities, reject the machine paradigm reflected in every part of their organization, and then commit to making necessary improvements.

His conclusion? "No, that won't work. We need a heavier hand to implement this because we don't have enough leadership influence to do it ourselves. We just need a playbook to tell people what to do so we can get moving faster."

In my head, I was thinking, "Rather than bring your peers on board, you think the answer is a book of instructions? Just tell people what to do, then they'll do it?" I understood his sense of urgency, but he wanted to abolish the problems caused by a machine paradigm with machine paradigm thinking.

He wasn't ready to shift his organizational paradigm, and it was clear that all he wanted from me was a checklist of things for everyone to do. We parted ways, and unfortunately, in the coming months, many of his company's employees left too.

This work is difficult. It requires you to fundamentally shift core ideas about high-performing organizations, and, ultimately, your own leadership performance. Getting rid of the flood is going to be messy and slow, and there is no perfect blueprint. I will tell you the same thing I tell every organization that I've ever worked with to stop the flood of organizational multitasking: *I know how to get started, but I can't predict what's going to evolve along the way.*

Ultimately, you will need to use the principles of flow to create your own organizational playbook. You don't need an army of expensive consultants to figure it out, but you do need time, effort, and persistence.

Take a Small Step First

AS YOU GET STARTED, EXPECT that the obstacles of wanting to change everything at once and finding a playbook to tell you how are going to be waiting for you. You might get stuck in them yourself, or they might ensnare others in your organization. But you have what it takes to avoid staying stuck. The way forward—and the way out of any trap—is to take a small step right where you are, with the imperfect organization you already have.

That small step could simply be making work visible by using a flow board. As you start to see the way your ecosystem currently operates, you'll be able to see the flood of multitasking and competing priorities. Making the flood more visible will almost instantaneously make it easier to see a part of the organization that is ready to limit work in progress and create flow.

Better Practices

WHILE THE OBSTACLES ARE VERY real, and you're likely to encounter them, there are some principles I want to share that will help you move past them. These are *better practices*—principles, actions, and patterns that reliably lead to improvement.

When it comes to creating more flow for yourself and the organization you lead—the kind of flow that leads to higher performance, more creativity, and happier people—letting go of the "best" way to do something is the only way you'll find the most effective way to actually do it.

Better > Best

The principles we explored in this book are a starting point. However, the specific way that your organization uses these principles will necessarily have nuanced differences from the way that every other organization puts them into practice. This is always true.

However, you aren't the first to navigate these challenges, and you don't have to reinvent any wheels. Even though your organization will need to experiment with the principles of flow, you can still learn from others who have already stopped the flood of organizational multitasking.

I can't tell you exactly what your better practices will become, but I can tell you exactly how to figure it out.

Let's return to the practice of Kanban introduced Chapter 5. Along with the physical practice of making work visible, the Kanban framework also offers four guidelines that can support you in your first steps toward flow. These guidelines can influence your choices about how to act, what to prioritize, and what to invest in, and they will help you find your better practices.[90]

1. **Start with what you do now.** When you make your current work in progress visible by creating an actual board, you are also creating an aerial view of your organizational ecosystem. You will start to see the many ways that the flood of multitasking is contributing to burnout and impacting your collective performance. You don't need to change ev-

ery process to find better flow—less flood and better flow is possible within your existing processes and organizational structures. In fact, starting with the organization you have is essential to identifying your next better steps.

2. **Agree to pursue incremental, evolutionary change.** Look for the simplest, smallest, and easiest place to make a change as a first step. Take one step forward, learn from what happened when you did, improve upon it, and then take another. A "big bang" change plan will *not* stop the flood—it will only make it worse. In actuality, evolutionary change allows you to take full advantage of one of our greatest assets as humans: our ability to learn and adapt. If everything changes at once, you'll overwhelm the system and slow down learning. The fastest way to restore the health of your ecosystem is through the momentum that comes from a series of consistent small changes, because some of those small changes will have an outsized impact on the outcomes.

3. **Respect current roles, responsibilities, and job titles *initially*.** Don't try to restructure everything at once by giving all your employees new job titles or by mixing up every team. If you find it necessary to do these things, do them down the road when your organization is no longer in a flooding crisis.

4. **Encourage acts of leadership at all levels.** This is by far the most powerful principle that will equip you to find better practices. If you are the leader of an ecosystem, your role is

to shape the environment so that it flows. That will empower people to do their best work, solve problems, and be better leaders—no matter where they are in the organization. And if you have leadership at all levels, you will not have to solve for everything on your own. Margaret Wheatley, who was one of the first to apply systems thinking to organizations, put it clearly: "I believe that the capacity that any organization needs is for leadership to appear anywhere it is needed, when it is needed." I couldn't agree more.

These guidelines don't tell you exactly what to do, but they can guide your decisions, help you prioritize where to start making changes, and help you find simplicity within your complex organization.

This isn't the only book you will need to be a great leader, nor will it solve all of your problems. But creating flow will make being a great leader and solving organizational problems easier. You can stop the flood of organizational multitasking and end the heavy costs that come with it. You can lead, *easier.* Doing better is absolutely within reach.

And, as I like to say, *better is always better than best.*

TAKE ACTION

Turn Real Flow into real work done. Check out companion resources at **realworkdone.com/book**

Get special pricing on bulk purchases by contacting **info@starblazerpress.com**

Invite Brandi Olson to speak at your next event or work directly with your organization at **realworkdone.com/our-work**

Be part of the conversation by following Brandi Olson on **www.linkedin.com/in/brandiolson**

Thank you for reading.

If you enjoyed *Real Flow*, help me connect with other leaders like you. Please leave a review on Goodreads or with the retailer where you purchased this book.

WITH GRATITUDE

FROM TIME TO TIME I'VE been gifted with an extraordinary question. There were two such questions that opened the possibility for this book. Illana Burk once asked me, "Would you ever consider writing about that?" It took me almost five years to come up with an answer. Along the way, Neil Ashvin Chudgar wondered, "Why do you care about multitasking so much?" At which point I realized that this book wasn't about productivity, it is about our human potential. With the gift of these questions, you both have shaped my understanding in remarkable ways.

In the process of answering those questions and many more, Rachel Allen, Kate Hefner, and John Schlimm helped me to find my voice as a writer and encouraged me to persevere. Alexis Rufi was exactly the research assistant I needed to get organized, and Molly Morrissey has diligently ensured I stay organized. Each of you had a unique role in helping me to get words on the page. Something I haven't always known that I could do.

And to Sam, Micah, and Nora who have given me the most honest of feedback on my stories and illustrations, my gratitude is the deepest of all.

ENDNOTES

1   W. Edwards Deming, *The New Economics for Industry, Government, Education* (Cambridge: The MIT Press, 2000).

2   Daniel Markovits, "How McKinsey Destroyed the Middle Class," *Atlantic*, February 3, 2020, https://www.theatlantic.com/ideas/archive/2020/02/how-mckinsey-destroyed-middle-class/605878/.

3   "The Illusion of Multitasking Boosts Performance," Association for Psychological Science, November 13, 2018, https://www.psychologicalscience.org/news/releases/the-illusion-of-multitasking-boosts-performance.html.

4   Paul E. Dux et al., "Isolation of a Central Bottleneck of Information Processing with Time-Resolved fMRI," *Neuron* 52, no. 6 (December 2006), https://doi.org/10.1016/j.neuron.2006.11.009.

5   Suk Won Han and René Marois, "The source of dual-task limitations: Serial or parallel processing of multiple response selections?" *Attention, Perception, & Psychophysics* 75 (July 2013), https://doi.org/10.3758/s13414-013-0513-2.

6   Dux et al., "Isolation of a Central Bottleneck of Information Processing with Time-Resolved fMRI."

7   Adele Diamond, "Executive Functions," *Annual Review of Psychology* 64 (January 2013), https://doi.org/10.1146/annurev-psych-113011-143750.

8   Diamond, "Executive Functions."

9   J. S. Rubinstein, D. E. Meyer, and J. E. Evans, "Executive Control of Cognitive Processes in Task Switching," *Journal of Experimental Psychology: Human Perception and Performance* 27, no. 4 (2001), https://doi.org/10.1037/0096-1523.27.4.763.

10 Dux et al., "Isolation of a Central Bottleneck of Information Processing with Time-Resolved fMRI."

11 Dux et al., "Isolation of a Central Bottleneck of Information Processing with Time-Resolved fMRI."

12 Rubinstein, Meyer, and Evans, "Executive Control of Cognitive Processes in Task Switching."

13 Diamond, "Executive Functions."

14 "Multitasking: Switching Costs," American Psychological Association, March 20, 2006, https://www.apa.org/research/action/multitask.

15 Gloria Mark, Victor M. Gonzalez, and Justin Harris, "No Task Left Behind? Examining the Nature of Fragmented Work," CHI conference 2005, https://www.ics.uci.edu/~gmark/CHI2005.pdf.

16 David M. Sanbonmatsu et al., "Who Multi-Tasks and Why? Multi-Tasking Ability, Perceived Multi-Tasking Ability, Impulsivity, and Sensation Seeking," *PLOS ONE* 8 (January 23, 2013), https://doi.org/10.1371/journal.pone.0054402

17 Jonathan B. Spira and Joshua B. Feintuch, "The Cost of Not Paying Attention: How Interruptions Impact Knowledge Worker Productivity," BaseX (September 2005), https://iorgforum.org/wp-content/uploads/2011/06/CostOfNotPayingAttention.BasexReport.pdf.

18 Silvia Bellezza, Neeru Paharia, and Anat Keinan, "Conspicuous Consumption of Time: When Busyness and Lack of Leisure Time Become a Status Symbol," *Journal of Consumer Research* 44, no. 1 (June 2017), https://doi.org/10.1093/jcr/ucw076.

19 Bellezza, Paharia, and Keinan, "Conspicuous Consumption of Time: When Busyness and Lack of Leisure Time Become a Status Symbol."

20 Ben Yagoda, "The Cognitive Biases Tricking Your Brain," *Atlantic*, September 2018, https://www.theatlantic.com/magazine/archive/2018/09/cognitive-bias/565775/.

21 Justin Cheng et al., "Break It Down: A Comparison of Macro- and Microtasks," CHI conference 2015, https://doi.org/10.1145/2702123.2702146.

22 Anna Love (CEO & Founder, Stoked), email message from author, September 23, 2021.

23 adrienne maree brown, *Emergent Strategy: Shaping Change, Changing Worlds* (Oakland: AK Press, 2017).

24 "Tittabawassee River Discharging at 374K Gallons Per Second, 23 Times Higher Than the Average," WXYZ, May 20, 2020, https://www.wxyz.com/ news/tittabawassee-river-discharging-at-374k-gallons-per-second- more-than-4-times-previous-record.

25 "Burn-out an 'occupational phenomenon': International Classification of Diseases," World Health Organization, May 28, 2019, https://www.who. int/news/item/28-05-2019-burn-out-an-occupational-phenomenon- international-classification-of-diseases.

26 "The Employee Burnout Crisis," Kronos, 2018, https://www.kronos.com/ resource/download/23811.

27 "The Employee Burnout Crisis."

28 Ashley Abramson, "Burnout and stress are everywhere," *Monitor on Psychology* 53, no. 1 (January 1, 2022), https://www.apa.org/ monitor/2022/01/special-burnout-stress.

29 "The Employee Burnout Crisis: Study Reveals Big Workplace Challenge in 2017," BusinessWire, January 9, 2017, https://www.businesswire.com/ news/home/20170109005377/en/The-Employee-Burnout-Crisis-Study- Reveals-Big-Workplace-Challenge-in-2017.

30 Peter F. Drucker, *The Effective Executive: The Definitive Guide to Getting the Right Things Done* (New York: Collins, 1967).

31 Shane McFeely and Ben Wigert, "This Fixable Problem Costs U.S. Businesses $1 Trillion," Gallup, March 13, 2019, https://www.gallup. com/workplace/247391/fixable-problem-costs-businesses-trillion. aspx#:~:text=The%20cost%20of%20replacing%20an,to%20%242.6%20 million%20per%20year.

32 "Table 18. Annual quits rates by industry and region, not seasonally adjusted," U.S. Bureau of Labor Statistics, updated March 10, 2022, https:// www.bls.gov/news.release/jolts.t18.htm.

33 "Opportunity Cost," Econlib, accessed April 6, 2022, https://www.econlib. org/library/Topics/College/opportunitycost.html.

34 Steve Blank, "Organizational Debt Is Like Technical Debt -- But Worse," *Forbes*, May 18, 2015, https://www.forbes.com/sites/

steveblank/2015/05/18/organizational-debt-is-like-technical-debt-but-worse-2/?sh=724ccof57b35.

35 Deming, *The New Economics for Industry, Government, Education.*

36 Shawn Achor and Michelle Gielan, "The Data-Driven Case for Vacation," *Harvard Business Review*, July 13, 2016, https://hbr.org/2016/07/the-data-driven-case-for-vacation.

37 TurnKey Vacation Rentals, "Leaving Work Behind – How U.S. Travelers Disconnect on Vacation," TURNKEY Blog, accessed March 17, 2022, https://blog.turnkeyvr.com/leaving-work-behind-on-vacation/.

38 Hayley Tsukayama, "Volkswagen silences work e-mail after hours," *Washington Post*, December 23, 2011, https://www.washingtonpost.com/business/technology/volkswagen-silences-work-e-mail-after-hours/2011/12/23/gIQAz4HRDP_story.html.

39 Nicole Lyn Pesce, "How Goldman Sachs and Citi are dealing with COVID burnout: Zoom-free Fridays and work-free Saturdays," MarketWatch, updated March 27, 2021, https://www.marketwatch.com/story/how-goldman-sachs-and-citi-are-dealing-with-covid-burnout-no-zoom-calls-on-fridays-and-no-work-on-saturdays-11616678936; Hugh Son, "Goldman's Junior Bankers Complain of Crushing Workload amid SPAC-Fueled Boom in Wall Street Deals," CNBC, updated March 18, 2021, https://www.cnbc.com/2021/03/18/goldman-sachs-junior-bankers-complain-of-crushing-work-load-amid-spac-fueled-boom-in-wall-street-deals.html.

40 Soo Youn, "America's workers are exhausted and burned out," *Washington Post*, June 29, 2021, https://www.washingtonpost.com/business/2021/06/28/employee-burnout-corporate-america/.

41 Ben Wigert and Sangeeta Agrawal, "Employee Burnout, Part 1: The 5 Main Causes," Gallup, July 12, 2018, https://www.gallup.com/workplace/237059/employee-burnout-part-main-causes.aspx.

42 Laura Powers (Chief Operating Officer, Business Agility Institute), video interview, September 15, 2021.

43 Sam Gustin, "The Fatal Mistake That Doomed BlackBerry," *Time*, September 24, 2013, https://business.time.com/2013/09/24/the-fatal-mistake-that-doomed-blackberry/.

44 "high performance," *Merriam-Webster*, accessed March 17, 2022, https://www.merriam-webster.com/dictionary/high%20performance.

45 Marcus Buckingham, *One Thing You Need to Know: About Great Managing, Great Leading, and Sustained Individual Success* (New York: Free Press, 2005).

46 Fritjof Capra, *The Way of Life: A New Scientific Understanding of Living Systems* (New York: Anchor Books, 1996).

47 Capra, *The Way of Life*.

48 Capra, *The Way of Life*.

49 Stephannie L. Lewis (Associate Vice President—Community Impact, Greater Twin Cities United Way), video interview, August 25, 2021.

50 Eliyahu M. Goldratt and Jeff Cox, *The Goal: A Process of Ongoing Improvement* (Great Barrington, MA: North River Press, 2012).

51 Goldratt and Cox, *The Goal*.

52 "NUMMI," *This American Life* podcast, episode 561, July 17, 2015.

53 Bradford H. Gray, Dana O. Sarnak, and Jako S. Burgers, "Home Care by Self-Governing Nursing Teams: The Netherlands' Buurtzorg Model," The Commonwealth Fund, May 2015, https://www.urban.org/sites/default/files/publication/53626/2000250-Home-Care-by-Self-Governing-Nursing-Teams-The-Netherlands'-Buurtzorg-Model.pdf.

54 "In First Person: Jos de Blok," SHRM Executive Network, Winter 2021, https://www.shrm.org/executive/resources/people-strategy-journal/winter2021/pages/in-first-person-de-blok.aspx.

55 René Descartes, *Discourse on the Method of Rightly Conducting Reason, and Seeking Truth in the Sciences* (Chicago: Open Court Publishing, 1910).

56 Capra, *The Web of Life*, 30.

57 Frederick Taylor, *The Principles of Scientific Management* (New York: Harper & Brothers, 1911).

58 W. Edwards Deming, *The New Economics for Industry, Government, Education*.

59 David Shultz, "The Effect of Coral Bleaching Events in the Great Barrier Reef," Eos, May 31, 2019, https://eos.org/research-spotlights/the-effect-of-coral-bleaching-events-in-the-great-barrier-reef.

60 Jen Roelke (Senior Director, Digital Team Engagement, Mayo Clinic), video interview, September 21, 2021.

61 "OKRs are Old News," *First Round Review*, September 1, 2016.

62 Donald Sull, Rebecca Homkes, and Charles Sull, "Why Strategy Execution Unravels—and What to Do About It," *Harvard Business Review*, March 2015, https://hbr.org/2015/03/why-strategy-execution-unravelsand-what-to-do-about-it.

63 "Kanban," Agile Alliance, accessed May 2022, https://www.agilealliance.org/glossary/kanban/.

64 Lace M. Padilla et al., "Decision making with visualizations: a cognitive framework across disciplines," *Cognitive Research: Principles and Implications* 3, no. 29 (December 2018), https://www.doi.org/10.1186/s41235-018-0120-9.

65 Marie Dingess (Agile Portfolio Lead, Capital One), email message to the author, September 24, 2021.

66 Veena Lakkundi (Senior Vice President, Chief Strategy Officer and Technology, 3M), email message to the author, September 22, 2021.

67 Mike Rother, *Toyota Kata: Managing People for Improvement, Adaptiveness and Superior Results* (New York: McGraw-Hill Education, 2009).

68 Ziva Kunda, "The case for motivated reasoning," *Psychological Bulletin* 108, no. 3 (1990), https://doi.org/10.1037/0033-2909.108.3.480.

69 Carolyn Ramsey (Senior Director, Talent, Digi-Key), email message to the author, September 14, 2021.

70 "Pareto Principle," Investopedia, updated December 25, 2020, https://www.investopedia.com/terms/p/paretoprinciple.asp.

71 Alan Jechort (Senior Software Engineering Manager, Blackbaud), video interview, August 18, 2021.

72 Andrew Means (Senior Director, Global Impact Data and Analytics, Salesforce), email message to the author, September 28, 2021.

73 Jim Ollhoff and Michael Walcheski, "Making the Jump to Systems Thinking," The Systems Thinker, accessed March 17, 2022, https://thesystemsthinker.com/making-the-jump-to-systems-thinking/.

74 Margaret J. Wheatley, *Finding Our Way: Leadership for an Uncertain Time* (Oakland, CA: Berrett-Koehler, 2007).

75 Scott D. Anthony et al., "Breaking Down the Barriers to Innovation," *Harvard Business Review*, November–December 2019, https://hbr.org/2019/11/breaking-down-the-barriers-to-innovation.

76 Diamond, "Executive Functions."

77 Adam Grant (@AdamMGrant), Twitter, December 31, 2019, https://twitter.com/AdamMGrant/status/1212024211616804864.

78 Anna Love (CEO & Founder, Stoked), email message to the author, September 23, 2021.

79 Phil Wahba, "Only 19: The lack of Black CEOs in the history of the Fortune 500," *Fortune*, February 1, 2021, https://fortune.com/longform/fortune-500-black-ceos-business-history/.

80 "Study: White Ex-Cons Chosen Over Blacks," CNN Money, June 17, 2005, https://money.cnn.com/2005/06/17/news/economy/hiring_bias/.

81 Victor Ray, "Why So Many Organizations Stay White," *Harvard Business Review*, November 19, 2019, https://hbr.org/2019/11/why-so-many-organizations-stay-white.

82 Kenneth Jones and Tema Okun, "White Supremacy Culture," 2001, http://www.cwsworkshop.org/PARC_site_B/dr-culture.html.

83 Jones and Okun, "White Supremacy Culture."

84 Aysa Gray, "The Bias of 'Professionalism' Standards," Stanford Social Innovation Review, June 4, 2019.

85 Peter Drucker, *Landmarks of Tomorrow: A Report on the New Post Modern World* (New York: Harper, 1959).

86 Peter Drucker, Management Challenges for the 21st Century (London: Routledge, 2012), 116.

87 "The Importance of Having a Cross-Disciplinary Team," Cornell Tech, June 23, 2016, https://tech.cornell.edu/news/the-importance-of-having-a-cross-disciplinary-team/.

88 Lisa Knapp (Senior Interactive Project Manager, Web Customer Experience Team, Room & Board), video interview, September 22, 2021.

89 Malcolm Gladwell, *Outliers: The Story of Success* (New York: Little, Brown and Co., 2008), 184.

90 "What is Kanban? Overview of the Kanban Method," Digité, accessed March 17, 2021, https://www.digite.com/kanban/what-is-kanban/.

CPSIA information can be obtained
at www.ICGtesting.com
Printed in the USA
LVHW110153201222
735599LV00004B/183